READING
TAROT

FIND YOUR INNER
FORTUNE TELLER
THROUGH THE CARDS

+ + ✦ + +

APRIL WALL

weldon**owen**

CONTENTS

+ + ✦ +

CHAPTER ONE

THE HISTORY OF TAROT AND PREPARING FOR A READING

HAVE YOU EVER seen someone reading tarot cards and thought it looked too complicated? Perhaps you've purchased a book in the past to learn and gave up midway because the language was too stuffy or the references were outdated. Maybe you've only heard of the word *tarot* before picking up this book and just want to see what all the hubbub is about. No matter what brings you here, I believe the information contained within this book will take you from curious bystander to everyday mystic in no time.

Now, more than ever, tarot can be found almost anywhere. No longer hidden in the shadows, divination in all its forms is enjoying a resurgence like never before. What our ancestors may have been burned at the stake for can now make you popular and much sought-after. From social media to your local library, tarot readers are plunging into the mysteries, secrets, heartaches, and joys of their friends, family, and coworkers' lives. All of this is happening with one simple tool—a deck of seventy-eight illustrated cards that covers life's struggles and triumphs. While the cards can deal with difficult and secretive topics, learning how to read them doesn't have to.

Tarot card reading, or cartomancy, is taken from the French word *carto*, meaning "card," and the Greek suffix *mancy*, meaning "divination." It is the divinatory art of discerning answers to life's questions through the use of a seventy-eight-card system. For years, I've performed tarot card readings for clients in search of answers. It is one of the many tools I employ as a psychic medium to help my sitters receive the information they seek. I learned at the knee of the strong women in my family who read countless tarot spreads. Fortune-telling, or *dukkering* as it is known in the Romany language, is one of the main ways my people were able to make a living while moving from place to place. As both Romany and a psychic medium, I find tarot card reading to be a special tool. The Romany not only helped spread this practice but also firmly put our stamp on it. In fact, every Hollywood movie you have ever seen featuring a tarot card reading probably involves a Gypsy stereotype (the term *Gypsy* is considered a slur and should not be used by non-Romany people). With this book, my goal is to not only teach you about the divinatory art of tarot card reading but also offer a true account of the Romany people and our role within this field. Though we helped popularize this art, it is not exclusive to our culture. Tarot card reading is *not* a closed practice. It is open to all those who come to it seeking answers. In fact, my ancestors would love nothing more than to know this beautiful tradition continues to be enjoyed.

So, what is so special about this set of cards? Well, it's been around for at least five hundred years, helping scores of people avoid tragedies, heal from broken hearts, and prepare for the abundance coming their way. Within the seventy-eight cards, almost every area of life is covered, from highs and lows to joys and sorrows. Reading these cards brings clarity to many situations. Could it be coincidence? Can it work only if the reader is "gifted"? Is it an evil practice? The answer to all of these is no! The truth is always found within the cards, but there is an unseen force that helps guide their selection. I refer to this force as Spirit. You may call it Source, a Higher Power, or God. All can be used interchangeably. But it is in the meeting of the mystical and the mundane that the magic of tarot takes place.

In the following pages, you will find all the information you need to become a reader of the cards. I have structured this book to take you through the process step by step, with each chapter building upon the previous one.

THE HISTORY OF TAROT

Even today, tarot's origins continue to be almost as mysterious as their use. There are no concrete dates or definitive countries of origin, but there is a general consensus regarding the humble beginnings of this powerful divination tool. Playing cards first appeared in fourteenth-century Europe. It was through traditional playing cards that suits were formed to break the deck into different categories. One early version was Clubs, Coins, Swords, and Cups. Those still bear a striking resemblance to the current four suits of tarot: Wands, Pentacles, Swords, and Cups. In addition to the four suits, the first documented tarot decks included additional trump cards with metaphorical drawings. Tarot was thus born from earlier playing card decks containing allegorical imagery, dating back to about the mid-fifteenth century and used in various areas of Europe. The deck's roots are said to be Italian and were originally known as *Trionfi* in association with the popular card game of *tarocchini*. However, it wasn't until the late eighteenth century that tarot became synonymous with the fortune-telling practice of cartomancy.

The current tarot deck is comprised of seventy-eight total cards, broken into two categories, the Major and Minor Arcana. The word *arcana* comes from the Latin word *arcane,* which means "hidden things or mysteries." So, the twenty-two cards of the Major Arcana represent the greater mysteries and secrets of life, the pivotal moments that challenge and reward us. The remaining fifty-six cards, known as the Minor Arcana, are split into four suits—Wands, Pentacles, Swords, and Cups—and represent the lesser mysteries of life, the more mundane, everyday issues we all face.

Jean-Baptiste Alliette (1738–1791), better known by his pseudonym, Etteilla, was a French occultist and the first to popularize tarot as a divinatory practice. He is known as the first professional tarot reader to earn his living by cartomancy. The next famous reader was Marie Anne Lenormand (1768–1830). She was the first tarot reader to the stars, rumored to be a confidante of Empress Joséphine of France. She was so popular and became so intertwined with the art of cartomancy that, following her death, a special deck was released in her name. Many people today still study the Lenormand style of tarot card reading.

Over the subsequent years, many decks became popular. One of the most common, and still used today, is the famous Rider-Waite Tarot Deck, which has been in print since 1909. It was named for the publisher, William Rider, and mystic A. E. Waite, who commissioned Pamela Colman Smith to illustrate the deck. The Rider-Waite Tarot Deck set the tone for the twentieth-century occult tarot used by mystical readers. This deck is now estimated to have over 100 million copies throughout twenty countries worldwide. Though many current tarot decks may look vastly different to the original Rider-Waite Tarot Deck, its symbolism and meanings are still considered an excellent foundation to build on. Because of its importance and serving as the standard measure for many modern decks to interpret, the Rider-Waite Tarot Deck is the basis for my visual descriptions in this book. In addition, the classic Rider-Waite tarot cards accompany the descriptions and explanations in the following chapters.

The spread and growth of tarot ran parallel with the movements of the Romany people. The Romany, a diasporic people who originated from India but had moved into Europe by the fourteenth century, practiced many divination arts, tarot chief among them. Who better to help sort out life's mysteries than a people who had traveled the world and who were wrapped in mystery themselves? Truly, we have been everywhere and seen it all. And through every place we have lived, we have intimately learned of the human condition. Although you may think a person in India has nothing in common with someone in England, you would be mistaken. The same issues, trials, troubles, and triumphs play out pretty much the same for everyone. Taking this knowledge in tandem with the Romany ability to make sense of life's mysteries made them front and center practitioners. The Romany are believed to have aided the spread of tarot card reading by conducting readings in parlors, private residences, and within their own *vardos* (wagons). Since they traveled extensively, the practice spread from Italy to the rest of Europe by the late eighteenth century.

PREPARING FOR A READING

Before we get started on the steps involved in a reading, a note about the language that will be used throughout this book. The person receiving a reading will be referred to as the *querent, client,* or *sitter* interchangeably. Also, the person giving the reading will be known as the *reader* or *seer*. I will also refer to people as individuals, sitters, clients, or persons. If I do reference someone in the singular, I will use the words *she* or *her* to keep the language from becoming clumsy.

STEP 1: SELECTING A DECK

First things first—time to get a deck. Let me go ahead and dispel a popular misconception about selecting a tarot deck for yourself. You do not—I repeat, you *do not*—have to be gifted or handed down a tarot deck in order to get started reading. I am unsure how this myth got started, but it is an unfortunately pervasive misunderstanding that floats around the internet. In certain families of readers, decks can be passed down. To receive a beloved deck is an honor, but it is *not* necessary. Also, friends, or those who know you have an interest, may buy you decks, but again, this is not a special initiation you must go through in order to be "worthy" of tarot.

Let me also make a note here about the differences between tarot and oracle decks. Because both tarot and oracle cards are popular right now, it is important to know they are separate divination tools and cannot be used interchangeably. Tarot is a seventy-eight-card traditional system of structure that has defined meanings, while oracle cards can vary widely from deck to deck in content and meaning. Think of tarot cards as your straight-to-the-point friend who gives you the truth—even when it might be painful to hear—and oracle cards as your mom who essentially tells you the same thing but wraps it up in a soft hug and your favorite snack. These two divination tools can work together, something we'll get to later in this book, but for now, we're focused on getting to know the tarot and all of its attributes.

So, if you are in need of a tarot deck before you start reading, let's talk about how to choose one. First of all—and you will hear this from me a lot throughout this book—use your intuition. Go to your favorite bookstore (even the big chains) and make a beeline to the mind, body, and spirit section. This can be found near self-help, psychology, or even religious areas in bookstores. Let your eyes take in the selection and pay attention to any decks that jump out at you. When you pick one up to read over the cover and get a closer look, notice how you feel when you do. Is there any change in your breathing? How about your heart rate? Do you feel flush or chilled? Goosebumps maybe? Your body is a great barometer for finding the deck that will work for you. On a practical level, you will probably want to find a deck that comes with an instruction booklet, as each deck's illustrator and author can tweak the cards' meanings and presentation.

STEP 2: PREPARING AND CLEANSING A DECK

Once you get your tarot deck home, it will need to be prepped and cleansed. There is already a kinship forming between you and your tarot deck by virtue of you buying it. Something gave you that tingly sensation, and you knew you had to have it. So, building on that, you want to match your vibration with that of the cards. This can be done in a number of ways, but here are a few to try.

Start by placing your hand a few inches above the deck. Hold it there and notice any changes in your palm. There might be a warmth that forms or waves of energy that you feel. While doing this, it may be helpful to close your eyes and set your intention for this deck. It can be as simple as: *I intend for this deck to be used to meet the needs of my clients* or *Spirit; please guide these cards to meet their highest and truest aim.* It is up to you how verbose or flowery you want to make the language. Again, it is all about putting your energy into the deck, and the deck reflecting that back to you.

You can also hold the deck against your heart space. Again, an incantation while you're doing this can help sync up the energies. Alternatively, you can touch the deck to your third eye (forehead) and pay attention to any sensations you receive.

These are only suggestions. If you feel like doing something entirely different, follow that instinct. The more you use your intuition, the better it will get, and having a honed intuition will only aid you in your future readings.

Now that you have a deck and your energies have harmonized, let's cleanse it. This is another step that can be done in a number of ways. I love to use dragon's blood incense smoke as a cleansing modality. Sage, palo santo, blessed water, or crystals can also be used to remove any lingering energies from the cards and make them a blank slate. Be mindful with the use of sage, palo santo, and any other culturally specific cleansing tool; it is important to appreciate others' cultures and not appropriate. If you are concerned with your use of certain products, use something else instead. Remember, using your favorite incense can do the trick just as well.

If you use a product that produces smoke, encircle the cards a minimum of three times in a clockwise fashion. If more feels better to you, do it. When using blessed water, take a cloth and dab a small amount on to it. Then, using the cloth, wipe the deck while the cards are still in the box. There is no need to soak them. In fact, it might be pretty difficult to read soggy tarot cards. If you want to use a crystal, use a clear quartz or selenite and let it rest on top of the deck for at least twenty-four hours. You can even use a full moon to clean your cards. Set them outside during the full moon. As they soak up the rays of the moonlight, the cards are cleared of any energy still attached to them. How to proceed is up to you. Let your intuition guide the way. Try a couple of different options, and find out which works best for you.

Once you have your deck cleansed, store it in a way that keeps it clear for you to work with in the future. Some people like to keep their tarot cards in a special bag, made from velvet or silk. Others keep theirs in a container, such as a wooden box. I prefer the velvet bag for the deck I'm working with the most. Inside the bag and resting on top of the deck, I place a clear quartz as extra cleansing and protection for the cards. Find out what works for you, and go for it. Most decks now come in attractive packaging, and you may feel comfortable letting the cards stay in there until you need them. It is important to note that energy builds with each use of the cards. With that in mind, cleanse your deck after each reading so that it can be reset and ready for the next time.

STEP 3: PREPARING YOURSELF AND YOUR SPACE

You now have your tarot deck, and it's prepared and cleansed. Now it's time to get you and your reading space prepared. First, find a space in your home in which you feel comfortable performing readings. This can be anywhere from a closet floor to an in-home office. Decorate it as ornately or as simply as you choose. You can add an altar with candles, incense, and pictures of loved ones in spirit, ancestors, and deities. The name of the game is always going to be what feels most comfortable to you.

Once you have your space picked out and decorated to your liking, cleanse it as much as you did your tarot cards. This also works for yourself. You can use smoking products, such as sage, palo santo, or incense. Walk through the space and let the smoke drift through the area. As it moves through, it is clearing the space of low vibration energies. You can also use Florida Water by sprinkling it throughout the space. Florida Water is an alcohol-based cologne originally used in the 1800s as a perfume. Since that time, it has been used as a spiritual cleansing aid, especially within hoodoo practices. Putting a little in your hands and rubbing them together can also help clear energies from you before a reading. Tulsi (holy basil) can be found in spray form and is also used to cleanse your space and yourself. Crystals can be placed within the corners of the rooms to help lift the vibrations as well as clear the area.

STEP 4: USING YOUR INTUITION

We are all intuitive beings. For some, it's a feeling in the pit of their stomach. For others, it is a knowing. For others still, it is a tiny voice in the back of their mind, telling them that something's off. Learning to stretch and grow those intuitive muscles is useful when reading tarot cards. The great thing about tarot is that you do not have to feel super psychic to begin. There are universal meanings for every one of the seventy-eight cards within the deck. When you're ready, you will feel twinges of intuitive information above and beyond the meanings in this book. You will start to fill in the gap between where the book's definitions end and what Spirit is impressing you with about your sitter's future. As with most things in life, this takes trial and error over time. Go easy on yourself.

CHAPTER TWO

CONDUCTING A READING

W HO'S READY TO start reading? Let's begin with the basics. When you're sitting down to do a reading, there are a few practical matters to work out. Before each reading, you may want to develop a ritual. This will not only put you in the right head space for a reading, but also signal to Spirit you're ready to work. From there, it's all about focusing on what you want the cards to tell you. Simply shuffle, select the right spread, and start reading!

STEP 1: CLEARING ENERGY AND SETTING AN INTENTION

Before conducting a reading, I light a stick of dragon's blood incense. This clears the space and works as an indicator to my spirit team that I am ready to work. I then set my intention for the reading ahead. I may use Florida Water or tulsi (page 9) to cleanse my own aura and raise my vibration. Another method of clearing away energy, and one that I use, is tapping on the deck before shuffling. I knock three times on the cards before proceeding. You can also blow on the cards to reset them. As mentioned earlier, the cards do accumulate energy with every reading, so it's necessary to cleanse them before each use. Some people like to tap the deck itself on the table a certain number of times. Find what works best for you. You can ask one hundred tarot readers how they prepare for a reading, and you'll probably get one hundred different answers. That's what's so beautiful about tarot card readings. It allows for so much personalization!

STEP 2: SHUFFLING THE CARDS
AND FORMING A QUESTION

Now you're ready to shuffle. Guess what? There are many ways to do this as well. When first getting started, you may want to follow a structured set of steps. You can riffle and bridge as you would with playing cards. You can simply pass cards from one hand to another. The choice is yours and should be something you feel comfortable with. A current trend is a quick and loose shuffling in which cards may fly out. Readers then take those freewheeling cards and use them as the cards meant for the reading. If that works for you, I say do it. Sometimes, readers will make a big pile of cards on the table and then pull random cards to make up the reading.

Regardless of the technique you end up using, focus on the question you want answered by the cards while shuffling them. If the reading is for another person, ask them to think about the question while you're shuffling. It is best to ask questions that require a full answer instead of yes or no. There are cards within the tarot that can indicate a simple yes or no, but that is a limited reading to give. Even when the sitter thinks she wants only a yes or no response, she will never turn down additional details. It is possible to do a general reading in which there is no guiding question—what comes up within the cards is the message for the sitter.

STEP 3: CHOOSING A TAROT SPREAD

When reading for yourself, set your intention, ask your question or be open to the general message, and shuffle the cards. Before beginning, decide which spread to use. A tarot spread is the arrangement of the cards, and this arrangement provides context for the reading. It guides the message you relay. Spreads can range from a single card to almost half the deck, if one is so inclined. Generally speaking, however, a spread will contain between three and ten cards. We'll take a look at some of the most common spreads used with real-life examples to follow to help you put it all together.

SINGLE CARD SPREAD

Let's begin with the easiest spread—a single card. Sometimes, all you need is a quick answer and laying down one card will facilitate that. Before pulling the card, set the intention for what the card will represent. It can signify your day ahead or a situation at hand in a quick, concise way.

**Day Ahead or
Situation at Hand**

THREE-CARD SPREAD

Perhaps you want a little more information. A simple three-card spread, albeit easy, is still informative. The cards, in order from left to right, can represent Past (previous events), Present (current situation), and Future (what will come to pass). A three-card spread can also take the form of What's at Hand (current situation), Obstacles to Overcome (difficulties affecting the situation), and Outcome (result). Again, use the spread that works best for your query.

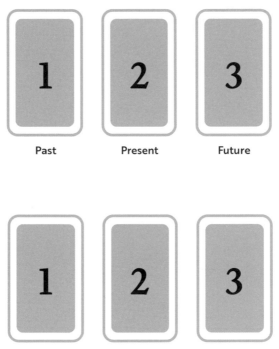

1	2	3
Past	Present	Future

1	2	3
What's at Hand	Obstacles to Overcome	Outcome

SIX-CARD SPREAD

Alas, you may find yourself needing even more detail. Never fear, another spread is here! When you're ready to take things up a notch, try your hand at a six-card spread reading. Again, you can decide what each card represents, but for the purposes of easing you into this process, let me show you one of my favorites. Don't be intimidated by the number of cards. Move to this type of spread at your own pace. Starting from the bottom row, reading left to right, there is Past Influences (what led to this point), Present Issues (current situation), and External Forces (outside people or events affecting the current situation). Moving up to the top row, the spread is completed with Internal Struggle (inner issues sitter faces), Something to Consider (different way to see the issue at hand), and What Will Be (eventual outcome).

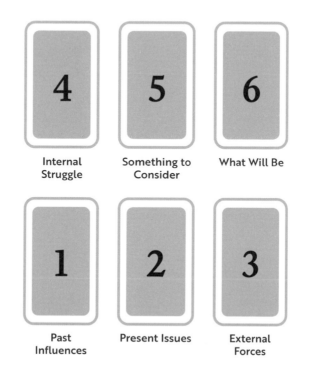

4	**5**	**6**
Internal Struggle	Something to Consider	What Will Be
1	**2**	**3**
Past Influences	Present Issues	External Forces

CELTIC CROSS

When you're feeling ready for an advanced reading, the Celtic Cross is a popular and long-standing spread. If your question cannot be answered with this one, it may need to remain a mystery for the time being.

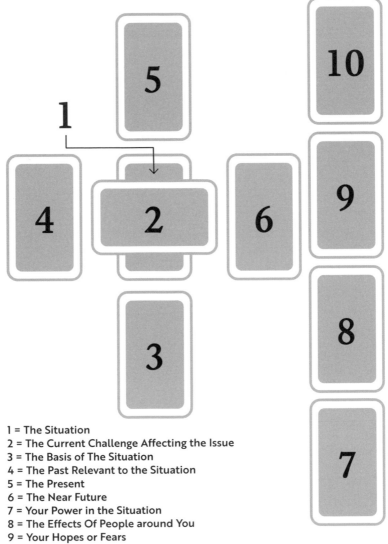

1 = The Situation
2 = The Current Challenge Affecting the Issue
3 = The Basis of The Situation
4 = The Past Relevant to the Situation
5 = The Present
6 = The Near Future
7 = Your Power in the Situation
8 = The Effects Of People around You
9 = Your Hopes or Fears
10 = The Outcome

STEP 4: GIVING A READING

Once the cards have been pulled and placed face up in the correct spread, it's time to get reading. Take a moment to survey the cards. What images pop into your mind? Do you feel any insights rise to the surface? How do they make you feel when you look at them? As you begin your tarot reading journey, you may want to keep a journal nearby and jot down your initial thoughts when seeing the cards.

With your cards in front of you, flip to the card meanings in this book. Apply the meanings based on the position they fall in within the spreads discussed earlier. It is your job to make a cohesive message out of the cards. When reading for someone else, ask the client to focus on a question or be open to a general reading, shuffle, and then lay out the cards in the preselected spread. Some readers will allow the client to shuffle the cards or at least touch them before reading them. If that speaks to you, incorporate it into your ritual. Once the cards are laid out, take in the entire scene. Notice how one card flows into the next. Although each card has its own individual meaning, it is your job to pull a consistent thread throughout the reading. Don't worry. The story will come together as you move from card to card. You can ask the client to let you know her question ahead of time, or if you prefer, after you have given your reading, ask if that answered the client's question.

When you first start, you will be nervous about getting it wrong. You may feel silly looking back and forth in a book for the cards' meanings. That is normal, and it is okay. Many people who are interested in getting a reading are completely forgiving of a new reader using the book. With time, much as an actor, you will also be "off book." Take your time and enjoy the journey.

EXAMPLE TAROT CARD READINGS

The following three sample readings are included to help familiarize you with real-life scenarios and their corresponding interpretations. Each spread will give you a hypothetical situation along with a full explanation of the tarot cards.

EXAMPLE 1: SINGLE CARD SPREAD

In our first example, let's say you're up for a big promotion, and you're eager to know if you will receive it. Rather than sweat it out waiting, you pull a single card to give you a heads-up on the matter. You shuffle the deck and turn over the top card. There sits the Sun (page 67).

First off, it is a Major Arcana card. That indicates an issue dealing with a big life event, such as a change at work. So far, so good. It is also upright. Things are moving in a positive direction. But what does the Sun card mean? From a quick skim of the keywords (page 67), the card's meaning is summed up as energized, success, and joy. That promotion feels closer by the second. This card is also a rare yes/no card and always indicates yes. So, in this case, you may want to start thinking how you'll celebrate, because chances are high you're about to take on a new title at work.

Keep in mind, however, that the tarot is not black and white. While everything about this card is positive, there is a chance the promotion still does not come through. Regardless, what you can take from this is that there is a good chance something even better is headed your way. Even when looking to the tarot for guidance, allow for life's little surprises. This way when a blessing in disguise appears, you, or your sitter, don't reject it because the outcome doesn't look exactly as imagined.

EXAMPLE 2: THREE-CARD SPREAD

Let's take a look at another scenario that would need more information than a one-card reading can offer. Perhaps your friend has been in a relationship for over a year and something doesn't feel right. She cannot quite put her finger on it, but she'd like to know where things are headed for her and her partner. After shuffling, you pull the following cards, from left to right: the Two of Cups, the Seven of Swords, and the Four of Wands.

The first card represents your friend's situation. As it relates to her question, pulling the Two of Cups signifies her relationship. The Two of Cups (page 120) stands for a deep connection and partnership. So, her relationship has a good foundation. There are strong emotions bringing these two together.

In the second position, the difficulties affecting her relationship are shown. In this reading, that spot is held by the Seven of Swords (page 107). This indicates that there is some deception within the relationship. While this can indicate infidelity, make sure your friend doesn't panic just yet. Deception can also take the form of hiding emotions or not being completely honest with one another. As this example shows, it is a good idea to assess all of the cards before jumping to conclusions.

The last card is the result, meaning if your friend can take the situation at hand and overcome the obstacles she's facing, this is most likely how things will turn out. For this spot, we have the Four of Wands (page 83). This is good news indeed. The Four of Wands means celebrations, more specifically weddings. It doesn't necessarily mean the two should fly to Las Vegas that night, but it is a hopeful result card to pull.

When taking this reading in as a whole, I'd say that since the outcome is so favorable and their relationship has a strong foundation, the obstacle of deception must not rise to the rank of infidelity, or at the very least be something both parties are willing to work through to find their happily ever after. Advise your friend to discuss her relationship concerns with her partner in an open and honest way. A thoughtful tarot reading such as this can offer insight and peace of mind.

EXAMPLE 3: SIX-CARD SPREAD

Both of the prior examples were pretty straightforward, but many times life is not. Maybe a client finds herself at a crossroads. It's not that everything's awful, but things could be better. Work is so-so; her love life is okay; friends and family are all well; but for whatever reason she feels stuck. So, her inquiry is more philosophical in nature. She wants to know if she is on the right path in life. That's deep, but let's see what the cards say about it. After giving yourself time to ruminate on this question and performing a thorough shuffle, these are the cards pulled.

The first card position represents Past Influences, and an upside-down Chariot (page 43) is drawn. The Chariot means movement, in control, and ambition. So, when reversed (page 44), this reflects a feeling of being out of control and stuck. Something in her past caused her to feel as if she wasn't in charge of her own

life. Moving to the second card, representing the Present Issues, another Major Arcana card is pulled in the form of the Hanged Man (page 53). This serves only to reinforce the client's feelings of stagnation. It is also clear when more than one Major Arcana card is pulled in a spread that the issue at hand is of great importance.

In the third spot of External Forces sits the King of Pentacles (page 151). Court cards generally represent a specific person in the sitter's life. This represents someone who is grounded, materially wealthy, and also willing to lend a hand if need be. Since this is in the External Forces position, it would seem someone in the sitter's life is available to help turn things around if she took the offer. Moving to the top row in the fourth card position is Internal Struggle, represented by the Eight of Swords (page 108). The Eight of Swords stands for feeling restricted and self-limiting beliefs. There are times in all our lives where we create our own prisons. It's easy to start to feel like there's no way out when our situation hasn't changed in a long time.

In the fifth position representing Something to Consider is the Eight of Cups (page 127). This card means walking away and endings. Perhaps the client needs to consider the option of starting over. If what's going on in her life isn't currently working for her, what's to lose by trying another route?

In the final position of What Will Be, the Ace of Swords (page 98) is pulled. This is exciting! The Ace of Swords, as with all Aces, brings the hope of new beginnings. This card, in particular, refers to breakthroughs and new ideas. That's welcome information indeed.

Let's put this all together now for the client. It is clear that she is feeling stuck and somewhat blah about life from the upside-down Chariot, Hanged Man, and Eight of Swords. However, there is help available to her if she can remove that blindfold and see it, metaphorically speaking. I would ask a client at this point if she's had someone offer her a new job or suggested some advice lately that she didn't take. Most likely she has, as that is what the King of Pentacles is all about. However, her own internal struggle of seeing herself as trapped is keeping her that way. I would tell her that Spirit is asking her to ponder what would happen if she walked away from her current situation and took up a new path. Does she really think it couldn't be better? In fact, based on the What Will Be card of the Ace of Swords, I would almost guarantee that she will soon find herself having a eureka moment and moving in an entirely new direction.

TAROT'S OTHER USES

While tarot is a timeless tradition, it is also versatile and flexible. That's the beauty of tarot. It can be used for so much more than just psychic readings. Let's explore some of those other avenues.

✦   Manifestation is the act of bringing something into your life through focused intention and inspired action. Tarot cards are excellent visual aids in helping you manifest. Once you've decided what it is you're wanting to bring into your life, go through your tarot deck and pick a card that represents it.

✦ Much like manifesting, spell work can be enhanced through the use of tarot. All magic begins with intention. So, for a simple love spell, you could use a red candle, a rose quartz crystal, rose petals, and the Lovers (page 41) or Empress (page 35) to call in the love you want in your life.

✦ Tarot can deepen messages when utilized with oracle cards (page 6). Set your intention to allow one oracle card to complete the message, and voilà: the reading becomes next level!

✦ A pendulum, which is a weight suspended from a chain to allow it to swing freely, can also be used with a tarot deck spread out. Gently guide the pendulum over the cards. When the pendulum begins to swing, select that card. Repeat this until you have the necessary number of cards for your spread.

REVERSED CARDS

When reading tarot cards, some may be pulled upside down. Some readers choose to read those and give them inverted meanings from the upright versions, while other readers use the upright meanings regardless of the card's orientation. Reversed meanings are not necessarily negative. Sometimes a reversed card can indicate too much of a good thing.

It is your choice whether to read reversals. Personally, I do not read them, as there is much variety already contained within the seventy-eight tarot cards in their upright positions. There are cards that represent positive moments and those that represent the darkest days of your life. I believe almost every situation in life is covered brilliantly just as the cards are, and I see no need to read upside-down cards. I simply shuffle in a way that ensures none are reversed.

When reversals are read, it can sometimes contribute a negative feel to the reading, which may induce unnecessary stress for the recipient. Again, this is your choice, and I strongly encourage you to determine for yourself what will work best for your reading style. Reversed meanings have been included so that you have the option to use them or not.

TAROT TIPS AND TRICKS

Over the years, I have picked up some helpful tips and tricks I'd like to share with you. Keep these handy as you're reading. They may help you out of a sticky situation or answer a question that pops up in the course of your practice. Also, jot down useful tidbits you learn along the way and compile your own tricks of the trade!

✦ You can strengthen your card-reading prowess by pulling a daily card to know what lies in store. Use a journal and write down your interpretations and predictions for the day. Each evening, go back to the journal and make notes about what you got right and what may have been misinterpreted. It is an excellent exercise to get to know the cards, their meanings, and your intuition.

✦ When first starting out, try tarot flash cards. Tape an index card to the back of the card and list keywords and notes that will help you remember the meanings. Get a friend to help you practice. You'll be surprised how fast you begin to remember the card meanings using this technique.

✦ When delivering potentially bad news or discussing an unpleasant topic, do so with tact and kindness. Avoid blurting out that someone's significant other is cheating or there is an upcoming death. Give an honest account of what the cards show in a way that does not add anxiety or stress to the client.

✦ Always advise a sitter that you **cannot** and **will not** provide medical diagnoses. Encourage the sitter to seek the counsel of a medical professional for all health-related issues. A tarot reading cannot and should not take the place of a medical professional's examination and opinion. This is also the case for mental health issues. If you decide to begin reading tarot professionally, keep a list of numbers or websites handy for medical and mental health providers, domestic violence and suicide prevention hotlines, and shelters as a resource for your clients.

✦ Nothing is set in stone, including the tarot cards. When someone gets a reading, it reflects a snapshot in time. Based on what the client does with that information, the situation can change. Be sure to remind your clients of this, especially if they seem concerned with the message they've received. The future is always fluid.

✦ Take the full scene into account before diving into a reading. One or two so-called negative cards does not necessarily mean the entire message takes a negative tone. Take care to not cause your sitter any undue stress or anxiety by expressing worry or concern at the appearance of certain cards in the spread.

✦ Make sure to never place personal judgments on the client's situation. Each of us is on our own journey. As a reader, it is your job to decipher the message, not deliver opinions.

✦ Trust that the cards pulled are exactly what the sitter needs to hear. It is tempting to pull additional clarifying cards, but oftentimes, that only muddles the reading. Believe in the process and the exact message needed will be delivered.

✦ If your energy is low or the cards are not making much sense, it is perfectly acceptable to postpone the reading until the conditions seem more favorable. Better to delay a reading than give an incomplete or inaccurate one.

✦ Just because a card may take on the appearance of a specific gender, the meaning behind it can be attributed to all genders.

✦ Be patient with yourself as you learn. Each reading is a step toward mastery. It does not all happen at once. And don't forget to have fun! Tarot can be mystical, spiritual, and exciting!

CHAPTER THREE

THE MAJOR ARCANA

THE TRUMP CARDS of the tarot, the Major Arcana, consist of twenty-two cards, beginning with the Fool (0) (page 29) and ending with the World (XXI) (page 71). The Fool represents the start of the tour through the tarot. Since no step has yet been taken, no number has been assigned. But the Fool is vital to tarot. It is his journey through the Major Arcana cards that introduces important life lessons and situations. His quest culminates with the World card in which the lessons have been learned and a new level of development has been achieved. This is known as the Fool's Journey, and the Fool represents each of us as we make our way through life. In the following section, the Fool's story will be woven throughout to help you understand the themes and meanings of each Major Arcana card.

The Major Arcana cards represent the big events in life—love, marriage, money, birth, death, downfalls, and resurrections. Within these twenty-two cards are life's biggest lessons, overarching themes, karmic influences, and archetypal characters. Again, these cards signify the greater mysteries of life. They embody those moments that can bring us to our knees or to our highest heights. For those who believe in reincarnation, the Major Arcana can be seen as those key points we need to take away from life in order to level up and either reach enlightenment, or at the very least, not have to learn certain lessons again.

Because the Major Arcana deals with the weightier issues of life, they are given more importance within a reading. When there is a majority of Major Arcana cards found in a spread, the sitter needs to pay attention, as life-altering situations and principal lessons are at play. Major Arcana moments can have bigger and more consequential effects on the sitter's life. For example, losing a job, getting a new job, death of a loved one, moving, or even the birth of a child are just a few of the possible circumstances the Major Arcana can allude to, as well as all of the life lessons contained within those moments. With a majority of the Major Arcana cards, the surrounding Minor Arcana cards (page 75) serve to add more details to the overall message. If most of the Major Arcana cards in a spread are reversed, the sitter may be ignoring or hasn't learned what Spirit is trying to teach, and thus the patterns continue to reappear in her life.

The descriptions of the Major Arcana cards that follow are based on the traditional Rider-Waite Tarot Deck reproduced in this book. However, the meanings and interpretations can be used with whatever deck you prefer. Although you may have a deck that is illustrated in a completely different way, the themes remain the same. Each card in this section is broken down into the traditional meaning as well as the interpretation for practical use within a reading. Let these be a jumping-off point for you. Over time and with practice, you will be able to add your own spin to each card's meaning.

0 - THE FOOL

Fresh start, new adventure, leap of faith, time for action

MEANING: The Fool begins the adventure of the tarot. It's the beginning, the start. The journey never begins without the first step. Do not be put off by the term *fool* to represent a person willing to take a risk. Yes, it can be foolish to step into uncharted territory. But most of our history and fairy tales are full of those same people who took that brave first step regardless of the risks and ended up triumphant. Put simply, the Fool is the origin of the Hero, and it's a role we can all play.

The Fool is perched at the precipice of change, screwing up the courage to take that leap. You cannot see what's beyond, but without movement you never will. A trusty pup is at the Fool's heels, excited for the road ahead or perhaps warning of the possible dangers. You will also notice that there is not much in the Fool's sack. How can there be? There is no way to pack for a trip one has never taken before. This card fully encapsulates stepping out on faith. There has to be an expectation that every step is still somewhat divinely guided and that the Fool will find footing once again. The sun is at the Fool's back, sending a warm supportive hug, pushing gently forward. The scenery set in the traditional Rider-Waite Tarot Deck indicates that this change will not come without possible obstacles or problems to overcome. However, what in life happens without some sort of struggle? How do we find ourselves if there's nothing to ever push against? This card hints that the prize is probably worth the risk. But again, you'll never know until you take a deep breath and dive in.

INTERPRETATION: In a reading, the Fool card can represent starting a new job, relationship, move, or any number of life events. Pay attention to where the Fool lands within the spread. Is it located in the Outcome spot or does it represent Past Influences that led to Present Issues (page 15)? This can indicate whether or not taking that leap of faith is warranted at this time. Also, the surrounding cards are important to give context as to whether or not the advice of this card should be followed. For example, if there are several other cards, such as the Four of Swords (page 103) or Five of Pentacles (page 141), which indicate right now is not a good time to start a new project or take a risk, then heed the majority's warning. This may represent how the querent is currently feeling—like they must set off on a new adventure. But is it necessarily what they need to do? Always look at a spread in totality to know the best course of action.

REVERSED MEANING: Hesitation, recklessness, take caution

THE MAGICIAN.

I - THE MAGICIAN

Inherent power, manifestation, ready for magic

MEANING: Hand raised high above, wand ready for the magic about to come, this is the Magician. This card represents the client and the potential within. It represents bringing forth something from the immaterial, or spirit form, into the physical, three-dimensional plane. Once the Fool takes the leap, how does he begin? Look at the table before the Magician. There lies a cup, pentacle, sword, and wand, each representing a suit (page 76) in the tarot deck. This alludes to the fact that the Magician already has all the tools needed to create magic. The cup represents emotions, the sword intellect, the wand passion, and the pentacle practicality. We are all guilty of looking outside of ourselves for magical solutions at times. This card reminds us that we have the power within, and whenever we so choose to act, we can. Look above the Magician's head. The infinity symbol is hovering there, right within the crown chakra. This is a reminder that we are all infinite beings with limitless potential. This is not some hokey, new-age concept. This is science. Energy can neither be created nor destroyed. So, the ability to tap into this unlimited source is available to us all. It is also important for the querent to know that all the pieces exist to put together to achieve whatever goal is at hand.

INTERPRETATION: In a reading, the Magician card represents the ability to manifest, to bring forth something new in the client's life. Due to this ability, things are probably about to get busy for the client. It is a reminder to not look to others for answers but to go within. If there are surrounding cards, such as the King of Pentacles (page 151), the World (page 71), or the Sun (page 67), the querent is ready to manifest abundance into reality. If the Empress (page 35) appears alongside this card, a child may be entering the picture as well. If there is a question weighing on the querent's mind that needs a definitive yes or no, the Magician is a resounding yes! Depending on where in a spread this card falls, follow the Magician's left hand pointing downward. This may give more information as to what the sitter can magically bring forward. This card overall serves as a pick-me-up to the sitter, reminding her that magic exists and, better still, it resides within her.

REVERSED MEANING: Insecurity, ineffective plan, misguided

II - THE HIGH PRIESTESS

Intuition, connection to Higher Self, divine wisdom

MEANING: If this chick doesn't have the answers, then no one does. The High Priestess is the meeting place between spirit and flesh, the magical point between two worlds, the gap between the mysterious and the mundane. She represents the Fool having realized he has all the tools he needs from the Magician but still doesn't know how to properly operate them. Enter the High Priestess. She represents the soul incarnate as a human being. She sits at the threshold of the mystical temple of Solomon, holding the scrolls of Tora, or divine law. She is in the know. She is truly at the midpoint between the seen and unseen, the light and dark. Behind her a curtain covered in pomegranates and palm leaves obscures the view. What hidden knowledge lies beyond? The moon is tangled in her robes, which appear to be flowing like a waterfall. Water is synonymous with intuition. It is that inner voice or gut feeling that keeps you from buying the wrong skirt or avoiding that sketchy guy at a party. It serves as protection that comes from the Higher Self, that part of us all that sits on a perch, able to survey our entire situation and guide us to make better choices.

INTERPRETATION: In a reading, this card represents the querent's innate ability to answer her own questions. The trick is getting still and quiet and hearing the whispers coming from the soul. Meditation would be good advice when this card appears. This could also represent a spiritual awakening for the querent. Dreams may be prophetic. New psychic powers may be developing, and this card is a sign of that, indicating that the client is on the right path. This card serves as a reminder that other people or places do not hold the answers the client is seeking. We all have the ability to tap into this wisdom, but accessing it does require faith and belief. The world is not black and white. True answers and wisdom lie between those two points, much like the High Priestess does on her throne. If the sitter is feeling frustrated or unclear about which way to go in a situation, or does not feel secure in trusting her own intuition, she can call on the wisdom of the High Priestess to help her reconnect with that part of herself. This card can be placed on an altar in order to strengthen those intuitive vibes within the sitter.

REVERSED MEANING: Unsure, rejecting one's spiritual nature, shallow understanding

III - THE EMPRESS

Divine Feminine, fertility, overflow

MEANING: Mother Earth personified, we revere you. All bow before the queen. She is the embodiment of the Divine Feminine. She brings forth life. She is the ultimate creator. It is this dynamic that will help the Fool start to bring forth the fruits of his labor. She wears a crown of twelve stars, signifying her connection to the earthly cycles of time (twelve months) and the heavens' guiding stars (twelve zodiac signs). She is a literal portal between two worlds. While the High Priestess card deals more with the ethereal and almost untouchable part of the spirit world, the Empress card makes manifest the spiritual into the physical. Every soul on this planet has passed through an empress to get here. She wears a robe of pomegranates, which invokes fertility. She sits upon velvet cushions, one of which is adorned with the sign of Venus, the universal sign of the feminine. This is the crunchy granola, earth mother card of the tarot. It does not get more maternal than this. She is backset against evergreen trees and lush grains at her feet. She is giving the most because she is the most.

INTERPRETATION: In a reading, a number of events can be indicated when the Empress card appears. First, if the querent is looking to get pregnant, foster a child, adopt, or look for a surrogate, this card is a great sign that those endeavors will be fruitful. If a real-life new human person is not what the querent is looking to bring into the world, then this card speaks to the creative spirit as a whole. The client may be about to birth a new project, such as a book, TV show, job, hobby, or any form of creativity. This card also speaks to abundance in many forms. If it shows up alongside a majority of Pentacles (page 136), then the abundance likely will be material (e.g., money). This card can also represent the client as someone who is either an earth zodiac sign (Virgo, Capricorn, or Taurus) or deeply connected to environmental concerns, a mama bear type, nurturing and body positive. If not a reflection of the sitter, then this card most likely represents a strong feminine energy in her life, such as a mother or grandmother. This card can also appear when someone is finally feeling at peace within their own body, both physically and spiritually. This is a chance to get back in touch with the Divine Feminine in one's life in order to provide balance when a situation calls for a softer touch.

REVERSED MEANING: Infertility, creative block, selfish

THE EMPEROR.

IV - THE EMPEROR

Aries, Divine Masculine, structure, authority

MEANING: The counterpart to the Empress, the Emperor card represents the father energy of life. Whereas the Empress is feeling and intuition, the Emperor is structure and rules, logic and reason. "Mother, may I?" gets met with "Wait until your father gets home." This energy will help guide the Fool in a more structured way. Stern-faced and a little uncomfortable atop his throne, the Emperor is not one to be toyed with. He is the master of his domain. He possesses a lot of the same characteristics as the rams that adorn his throne—persistent, determined, and sometimes hardheaded. The rams are no accident, as they represent his connection to the zodiac sign of Aries and the planet Mars. But the Emperor does have a role to play. Life cannot be led by the heart all the time. There needs to be a good mixture of thinking things through and letting reason be a guide in decision-making. The Emperor sits in full armor covered by a fiery red robe, indicating his passionate demeanor but also protective nature, for others as well as himself, where getting to his soft underbelly is difficult to do. He holds the ankh in his right hand and the globe in his left, representing the world in which he feels dominion over.

INTERPRETATION: In a reading, this card can represent the sitter's father, father-in-law, stepdad, or an authority figure, such as a boss. This person can be living or in spirit, as most of the cards that display people can be. Depending on where it falls in the spread, the sitter could be facing a situation where she feels dominated by a person or an issue. Perhaps there are father issues that need to be worked out. This card can also indicate being raised to the point of authority, such as a promotion at work or recognition by an important figure. Based on surrounding cards, such as the Seven of Pentacles (page 143) or Eight of Pentacles (page 144), the Emperor card can remind the client that structure is needed in order to accomplish the goal at hand. Conversely, the client may need to take a looser approach if playing by the rules has not reaped the benefits she was hoping for. Again, because this also represents the zodiac sign Aries, the querent may have some ongoing situation with an Aries in her life or be born under that sign herself. If that is the case, look to the accompanying cards to see what course she needs to take. The sitter may also display Aries traits, such as independence, leadership, and passion.

REVERSED MEANING: Immaturity, abuse of power, rage

V - THE HIEROPHANT

Taurus, teacher, spiritual leader, tradition

MEANING: The Hierophant sits in a similar manner as the High Priestess, but where the High Priestess goes within to seek knowledge, the Hierophant seeks it from established sources. There does not have to be a go-between for you to meet with the Divine, but it is helpful at times, especially when first starting out on a spiritual quest. The Hierophant appears in order to help guide the Fool further along his journey. The Hierophant sits in as the medium, the channel, to help guide an initiate. He carries the papal cross in his left hand to signify his connection with traditional spiritual beliefs and raises his right hand in a blessing, pointing heavenward. At the bottom of the card sit two followers, looking to be guided on the path of enlightenment. As both appear to be male, this card also speaks to the patriarchal history of religious orders. The Hierophant stands in as the gatekeeper. It is his job to pass down spiritual wisdom. At his feet are two crossed keys that signify the Hierophant's ability to unlock mysteries that he is qualified to teach.

INTERPRETATION: In a reading, this card can represent the querent's search for spiritual growth and development. She may be looking for a group of like-minded people to travel with and to learn from on her spiritual journey. Communal religious systems do hold value in that they give group support and a sense of belonging. When this card appears, it indicates that a teacher may be showing up to help guide the querent on her way. As the old maxim goes, "When the student is ready, the teacher appears." Alternatively, based on the cards present, such as the Six of Cups (page 125) or Judgement (page 69), the client may be dealing with old wounds or trauma from a spiritual upbringing that no longer resonates for her. She may be feeling disconnected from her faith altogether and is looking for something to fill that void. Many times, this card will appear when the client is a bit on the younger side, as most people begin to question their inherited religion once they are able to move away from home and begin to form their own opinions on the subject. Also, this card represents the zodiac sign of Taurus. So, it could be possible that either the sitter or someone close to her is born under this sign or exhibits the quality of a Taurus, such as hardworking and loyal, regardless of birth sign.

REVERSED MEANING: Blind faith, unorthodox, corrupt spiritual leader

VI - THE LOVERS

Gemini, relationships, union, love

MEANING: Sweet amore. This is what it is all about. That loving feeling. Soul mate vibes. Cosmic fated twin flames. So far, the Fool has been on his earthly journey all alone, but now enters a mate. The Lovers stand before the archangel Raphael, whose name means "God healed." When we fall in love, isn't that how we feel? Healed. As if what was missing has been found, and we are now whole. Even though we know our romantic partners are not there to complete us, it is nice to have at least one other human on this planet who really gets you. The man and woman are both naked, symbolic of revealing their true feelings. The sun beams down on them. Behind the woman looms the tree of knowledge with the snake still present, harkening back to the Garden of Eden. Behind the man stands a tree of twelve flames, representing passion, as well as the twelve signs of the zodiac. In the center rises a volcano, which is somewhat phallic in presentation and alludes to the eruption of passion when one is drawn to another. As the man gazes at the woman, she looks to the angel above. This illustrates the path of physical desires to emotional needs to spiritual truths.

INTERPRETATION: In a reading, the Lovers card is always a positive in regards to romantic pursuits. If the querent wants to know if the person she is with is a good match, the answer would be yes. The Lovers represent a balanced union, a complement to each person within the relationship. This is not a fling. This is the real deal. If the card appears before the Tower (page 61) in a spread, a breakup may be indicated. If it shows up in the Outcome spot (page 14), then the relationship is sure to be fated bliss. This card does not necessarily refer to only romantic partnerships. It could signal a positive work relationship or coupling that will benefit each party. Look to surrounding cards to clarify the meaning. The Lovers can also refer to a choice before the querent, one where both options look favorable. In this case, the client is advised to use her heart to make the decision, as it will not steer her wrong. The Lovers also represents the sign of Gemini and can identify either the client or someone close to her born under that sign. The sitter or someone close to her may exhibit Gemini traits, such as being quick-witted and curious. Also, she may be of two minds about a situation, and it is time to choose.

REVERSED MEANING: Break up, conflict, unrequited love

VII - THE CHARIOT

Cancer, movement, in control, ambition

MEANING: This is the first card of the tarot not focused on a person. Instead, this card emphasizes the mode of transport, the chariot. What comes to mind when thinking of a vehicle? Speed and ease of maneuverability. Just thinking about walking to a destination and my feet get tired. With the use of a vehicle, any journey becomes that much easier. Things are about to pick up for the Fool. A warrior stands tall within the chariot, guiding it forward through sheer will and seeming magic, as the wand in his right hand demonstrates. As you can see, there are no reins present. His eyes remain focused straight ahead, and he is determined to reach his destination. This card does represent the zodiac sign of Cancer. Much like Cancer, the warrior is protected by armor, but beyond that, he can be quite sensitive. One black and one white sphinx sit in front of the chariot, seemingly at odds, as each pull in opposite directions, but the driver is undeterred and continues to move straight ahead.

INTERPRETATION: In a reading, the Chariot is a great card to pull if the sitter has been feeling stuck and stagnant. This card is all about action, drive, and determination. The power and control are on the sitter's side, and she can guide her life in any direction she so chooses. Within a spread, this card can signify that, through hard work, the querent can get ahead. This can mark the start of a rather intense but short-lived period in the querent's life, such as the start of a new business, new job, or new educational experience. If the querent is somewhat shy and reserved, this card is a good reminder that sometimes not taking no for an answer is a good thing. Unlike the Wheel of Fortune (page 49), the client is in the driver's seat of the momentum about to enter her life. The Chariot does represent the sign of Cancer and so can reflect the fact that the client or someone close to her was born in June or July or exhibit the traits of Cancer—a hard exterior but warm and gooey interior, a homebody, and someone who is fiercely loyal and protective of family and friends. The best advice here is to get ready for the ride of a lifetime and to set off in whatever direction feels best.

REVERSED MEANING: Out of control, lack of direction, delay

VIII - STRENGTH

Leo, inner strength, patience, subtle power

MEANING: Now this card is neither represented by a person nor an inanimate object. Instead, it's represented by a quality. That quality is strength, defined as the capacity to withstand great force or pressure. Many times, we think of strength as a show of muscle, but that is not what Strength in the tarot is about. As things have intensified for the Fool on his journey, strength will be an important value to cultivate. As you can see from the card, there stands a woman stroking a lion. Although the lion is known as the king of the jungle in most circumstances, when it faces inner persistence and patience, the ferocious beast becomes a tame tabby. The lion represents passion and force. It can also stand for troubles in our life that feel too powerful to conquer. The woman, dressed in white flowing robes and adorned with a crown, is the true representative of strength in this depiction. The white of her gown speaks to her purity of heart and spirit. The crown she wears is made of flowers, pointing to a connection with nature and letting her inner self reflect naturally outward. She has not sought to forge a crown from hard metals or stones, but instead lets the flowers speak gently to her power to lead. The infinity symbol floats above her head, much like we saw in the Magician's card (page 31), and as with the Magician, the symbol alludes to the infinite potential for strength within the woman.

INTERPRETATION: In a reading, the Strength card symbolizes getting through a rough patch in life by staying steady and patient. This situation will not be overcome by yelling, screaming, or even running away, but rather with quiet fortitude. This card normally pops up when a client feels at the end of her rope with an issue and thinks she has no more left to give, but Spirit uses this card as a reminder that her ability to keep pushing is more resilient than even she knows. Depending on the other cards in the spread, Strength can represent that ultimately whatever the sitter is facing will be overcome. This card also represents the sign of Leo. That could be the sitter herself or someone she is inquiring about in the reading. This card can also reference Leo qualities, such as leadership, grace, and compassion, which may be required for resolution in the sitter's current situation.

REVERSED MEANING: Self-doubt, weakness, fear

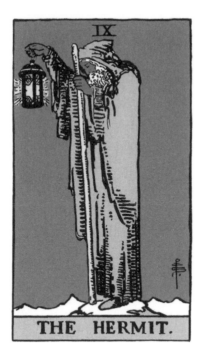

IX - THE HERMIT

Virgo, solitude, gestation, introspection

MEANING: Almost halfway through the Major Arcana, it makes sense to see a bit of a slowdown on the journey. The Fool has been dealing with some life issues and knows he is strong enough to see them through, but sometimes life requires a time-out to set things right again. The Hermit represents that inward gaze in the tarot. He stands on a mountaintop, surveying the road before him. In his right hand, he carries a lantern lit by a six-sided star, the seal of Solomon. In his left hand, he bears a staff, giving him balance. His path is lit, but only dimly so. This requires that he take some steps on faith, much like the Fool initially did on the start of his journey. However, now he is wiser and realizes that, while the road may be dark momentarily, eventually the sun will reappear. There is not as much trepidation from the Hermit. He knows he needs to check back in with himself to make sure the road he is on is still the one he wants to travel.

INTERPRETATION: In a reading, seeing the Hermit normally means the querent needs to do some self-reflection. If this card pops up when asking about potential romantic partners coming in, the answer is usually not now. This is a time of solitude and learning how to be comfortable with oneself. I have found that when someone enters a period of introspection reflected in the Hermit, soon after emerging back into the world, the love they were searching for will find them. There may be some recent events that need time to be processed by the querent. That should be encouraged. The Hermit also represents the zodiac sign of Virgo. The querent may be born under that sign or exhibit some of the Virgo traits, such as an eye for detail or putting others first. This card does not equal a time of loneliness for the sitter, just a time of being alone. If this card shows up along with the Six of Swords (page 106) or the World (page 71), it would be wise to take a solo trip. This could be to anywhere. The destination is not important as long as it provides some space for the sitter to be at peace. There is great wisdom to be gained from closing oneself off from the noise of the world, at least for a while, in order to recenter and regroup and find firm footing once again on this life's journey.

REVERSED MEANING: Extroverted, giving up, restlessness

X - WHEEL OF FORTUNE

Cycles, movement, opportunity, change

MEANING: So, after some introspection, it is time to get things moving again, and the Wheel of Fortune is all too happy to oblige. Unlike the Chariot (page 43), you are not necessarily in the driver's seat with the Wheel of Fortune, but that is okay. Sometimes we have to learn how to go with the flow instead of trying to dictate the way. The Fool is about to get an opportunity to apply some of that wisdom he learned while in isolation. There is a lot going on in this card. So, let's break it down. The wheel itself contains the Hebrew letters YHVH, which spell out the unsayable name of God, as well as TORA, referring once again to divine law, but have also been thought to refer to the word *tarot* itself, or *rota*, Latin for "wheel." In the center are symbols for mercury, sulfur, water, and salt, which are essential for life. Three creatures take up positions on the wheel itself. At the top is the sphinx, representing wisdom. Going down the left side is a snake, representing the Egyptian god Typhon, and near the bottom is Anubis, the Egyptian god of the dead. The fourwinged creatures represent the four fixed signs of the zodiac, which are Aquarius (the angel), Scorpio (the eagle), Taurus (the bull), and Leo (the lion). This represents different phases and seasons of life.

INTERPRETATION: In a reading, the Wheel of Fortune indicates change is coming and that it is best to go along for the ride. This represents the unending cyclical nature of life. What goes up must come down. When things are going well, you can bet that they will get bad for a time. Conversely, when things suck, good times are just around the corner. In terms of the interpretation of this card, a lot depends on the client's current life situation. She may not want to hear that things are about to change. She may be enjoying them just as they are. However, what choices the client failed to make in the Chariot part (page 43) of her life will now be fixed by the Wheel of Fortune. It is a way for the Universe to course correct. In many cases, the Wheel of Fortune is a welcome sight as the querent's life may be feeling off-kilter and this gives her a chance to get back on track. The Wheel of Fortune may be referencing a karmic pattern that is occurring to the querent as well. Instead of fearing it, the querent should see this as an opportunity to make a different choice this time around.

REVERSED MEANING: Moving backward, obstacles, missed opportunity

XI - JUSTICE

Libra, karma, legal issues, balance

MEANING: It is time for some wrongs to be righted. The Fool may feel like things have gotten a little out of balance and this is a chance for that to be rectified. Justice sits on her throne similar to the High Priestess (page 33) and Hierophant (page 39) flanked by two pillars, which represent balance and structure. In her right hand she holds a sword, representing logic and intellect, as the suit of Swords (page 98) does throughout the tarot. In her left hand, she holds the scales, representing a more intuitive approach to finding equilibrium. Peeking out from beneath her red robe is one white shoe, which speaks to the spiritual choices we all face. Justice is the midway point in the Major Arcana. Karmic debts have been collected and need to be handled. This is not a strict black-and-white issue of correction. It is more about equaling things out than meting out punishment. So, this card should not be feared but rather understood to be important in the grand scheme of things to help equal out a situation.

INTERPRETATION: In a reading, the Justice card can indicate legal issues for the client. These may be already known to the client or could be something on the horizon, depending on where it falls within a spread. Based on the surrounding cards, it can be determined whether the legal issues will or will not come out in the client's favor. Justice can also be advice that the sitter needs to take, as in doing what she knows to be right. We all have an inner moral compass, and this card reminds us to lean on that for decision-making. This card also represents the zodiac sign of Libra. The sitter or someone important in her life may have been born under this sign or exhibits Libra's qualities like fairness, intellect, and charisma. Where it pops up in the spread could also be a reminder that it is time for the sitter to be accountable for mistakes made. We all have the tendency to think of karma as something happening to someone else, but deep down, we know that is not true. What goes around comes around, and this card can represent karma being paid either by the sitter or someone who owes it to her.

REVERSED MEANING: Injustice, imbalance, bias

XII - THE HANGED MAN

Feeling stuck, surrender, incubation

MEANING: Sometimes you have to let it all hang out. The Fool has dealt with some karma and needs a fresh perspective, but before moving ahead, things might need to go a little topsy-turvy first. In the Hanged Man, you have just that. The person is held upside down from his right foot in a cross made from tree limbs, resembling the cross. His left leg is bent at the knee and tucked behind his extended right leg. His arms are folded behind his back. Take a close look at this face. Does he seem super stressed to be hanging from his heel? Not really, right? His face seems to be at ease and almost peaceful. His head is enveloped in a halo of golden light, which represents enlightenment and understanding. From that angle, the Hanged Man has a different vantage point on life. It seems as if he knows something we may not.

INTERPRETATION: In a reading, this card represents the pause button being hit on the querent's life. It could be self-imposed, but most times, it is outside the querent's control. This is a time of suspended animation. Not much seems to be happening. Meanwhile, things are going on in the background of the querent's life, although she may not be aware of it. When this card appears, it is a good moment to reevaluate the situation the client finds herself in. From upside down, the world certainly looks different. This card can indicate that a eureka moment for the client may be on the horizon, where she can see the solution to a problem with fresh eyes. If a question is asked regarding the start of something new or momentum, the answer is most likely no, depending on the surrounding cards. However, this is not wasted time. It's an incubation. Something is being formed to come into reality. Whereas the Hermit (page 47) is an active step back from the world, the Hanged Man is a booby trap set by Spirit to get the client to hold up before continuing to plow full steam ahead. If ever there was a period to surrender to the process, this is it. That does not mean it will feel great, but there will be meaning behind it—it's not a cruel joke that fate is playing on the client. Sometimes there is some discomfort for the overall greater good.

REVERSED MEANING: Taking action, movement, thoughtlessness

XIII - DEATH

Scorpio, change, transformation, ending

MEANING: Death is one of the most feared cards of the tarot—and one of the most deeply misunderstood. I dare say it shares a striking similarity with the zodiac sign of Scorpio, which it represents. The Fool is about to upgrade. This card depicts a pretty graphic scene, and so when sitters first see it, it can be jarring. However, once you know the actual meaning, it is less scary. Death is pictured seated on a white horse, carrying a black flag with a white rose of five petals. He is still dressed for battle, but only a skeleton remains. The number five is not arbitrary, as it represents change. Death comes for us all, as evidenced by the fallen person on the ground. Others can be seen with eyes closed, trying to avoid the inevitable. A religious figure stands in front with hands outstretched, seemingly pleading and also interceding for others. The sun sets low in the corner of the picture between two towers, which will appear again in the Moon card (page 65). The sun setting and rising each day is a tiny glimpse into the endings and beginnings theme of this card. While this is going on in the foreground, a boat quietly sails down the river in the background to signify that, while there are endings for some, new beginnings have just started for others.

INTERPRETATION: In a reading, this card signifies that the querent is going through some rough stuff, even though good stuff ultimately comes from it. So, depending on where it falls within a spread, Death can represent a breakup, a job loss, and in rare cases, an actual death of a loved one. The important thing to remember about the Death card is that endings are necessary for new starts. If we do not make room in our life for new energy, things become too stagnant. This is the logical next step in life once one has experienced the immobility of the Hanged Man. Change has to come, and we either go willingly or we fight against it—and suffer from it by extension. Growth comes when we realize life is cyclical. The Death card also represents the zodiac sign of Scorpio. Depending on where it falls within the spread, it can represent the querent or someone in her life born in October or November. The important thing to remember with this card is that, while there are changes happening, they are not altogether unexpected by the querent. They may have been coming for a while. Again, that does not make them any less painful. So, handle this card with care.

REVERSED MEANING: Stagnant, resisting change, stalled out

XIV - TEMPERANCE

Sagittarius, patience, balance, the middle way

MEANING: So, life may have suddenly shifted and changed, and things feel a little out of whack. What do we need to do in times like these? No, not day drink until we forget the past. As tempting as that might be, we need to work on balance, not extremes. The Fool has dealt with quite a bit up to this point, and Temperance comes in to help set things right, actually offering some help from above. In this card, an angel stands draped in a white robe with wings extended, pouring water from one chalice to another. This symbolizes the flow of the spiritual into the physical and the over-all flow of life. The angel stands with one foot in the water and one on the dry bank of the river. This represent the need to be in flow while also remaining grounded. It also suggests how angels can stand in the gap between the spiritual and physical worlds. This is the behind-the-scenes working of Spirit illustrated. Behind the angel is a trail leading up a mountain with a bright shining sun capping it off. This alludes to the journey of life that we are all on.

INTERPRETATION: In a reading, this card means that the sitter needs to find some balance and flow within her life. Even in the midst of chaos, it is important to realize that life has natural ebbs and flows, and it is our job to find the middle way between it all. Not too high, not too low. Just the right approach. This may be thought of as the Goldilocks card of the tarot. Depending on where this card falls in the spread, there may need to be a rebalancing within the sitter's life relating to relationships, career, or health. Also, Temperance represents the zodiac sign of Sagittarius. If the sitter herself is not a Sagittarius, someone important in her life may be or have Sagittarian attributes, such as funny and freedom-seeking. Alternatively, Temperance can be a message from Spirit that there is unseen help being sent at this time in the client's life. This may take the form of a guardian angel, guide, or loved one in spirit. That is why moderation is stressed in this card; there is no need to worry about or force a situation, as you never know what help may be coming from the other side.

REVERSED MEANING: Impatience, imbalance, overindulgence

XV - THE DEVIL

Capricorn, addiction, destructive behavior, toxic situation

MEANING: When areas of our life drift to excess, addiction and destructive behavior result. That is exactly what the Devil represents. The Fool did not heed the warning of Temperance and now faces the imbalances created by his choices. In this card, the Devil is represented by Baphomet, a half-man, half-animal creature that symbolizes a balance of opposites: both male and female, animal and human, and good and evil. At his clawed feet are two humans chained to the podium on which he rests. Although tethered, the chains around their necks are loose, appearing to be removable if either person attempted it. Similar to the winged Baphomet before them, each human bears animal-like qualities of horns and tails. In fact, their tails refer back to the Lovers card (page 41) with the pomegranate being attached to the woman and the flame attached to the man, an allusion to original sin. This card is like when a beautiful relationship goes toxic. We have all either experienced one of those or at least seen one take place. It is the embodiment of too much of a good thing.

INTERPRETATION: In a reading, this card reflects something holding the client back in life. This could be an actual addiction, such as drugs, alcohol, food, gambling, etc. It could also reflect the shadow side of the querent and there being an imbalance in their life, pulling them further into bad habits rather than appealing to their better angels. This behavior can show up as excess and indulgence. These lower vibe activities can make the querent feel trapped and beaten down. Ultimately, what the Devil means in a reading is that the querent is experiencing a disconnect from a higher power. In Christianity, there is a belief that hell is all about fire and brimstone and suffering for sins. But in actuality, it is all about separation from God because we all came from the same source and are interconnected. When we lose the ability to feel that connection, it turns us to other outlets in search of solace with which to fill that gap. The sitter is faced with some tough choices, but the good news is that this situation does not have to become permanent. Again, as the chains are freely hanging around the humans' necks, they had a hand putting them there and they can be empowered to remove them. This card also represents the zodiac sign of Capricorn. So, the sitter may have been born under that sign or she could be exhibiting some of the shadow sides of that sign, such as overworking or becoming too materialistic.

REVERSED MEANING: Liberation, improving situation, healthier lifestyle

XVI - THE TOWER

Destruction, upheaval, turbulence

MEANING: When the Tower shows up, the excesses of the Devil (page 59) have gone too far. Things are now falling apart. The Fool is not enjoying this leg of the journey, but it is an important part. In the heat of things, however, that is often difficult to see. The card depicts a lone tower high on a rocky mountaintop. Lightning strikes its crown, a literal crown as well as a symbol for the crown chakra, the connection between the spiritual and the physical. Two people are falling out of the tower headfirst. In the air floats twenty-two individual flames, representing the twelve zodiac signs and ten points of the Tree of Life. There is mass panic and chaos represented in this card. A lightning strike is not something that can be forecast. It happens quickly and with great power. Most times, however, there is a storm brewing before it hits. Distant thunder can be heard rumbling for a while before the lightning strikes. The same holds true for the Tower. Things have gotten bad, but it is probably not a complete surprise.

INTERPRETATION: In a reading, depending on the placement, this card can represent a tragedy for the client that has occurred, is occurring, or will occur in the future. This is the big life stuff that no one likes dealing with—death, job loss, cheating, homelessness, serious illness. To put it bluntly, these are the moments in life that can bring you to your knees. There is always a silver lining, however. Spirit never leaves us without help. The best thing to remember about this card is that sometimes life has to fall apart in order for things to be built back up. This is a fire sale, everything must go. This is a true test of surrendering to the flow of the Universe. Many times, this card can pop up during someone's spiritual awakening. Unlike the love and light illusion of new-age spiritualism, an awakening can be quite intense. In a sense, the image of what one felt life was supposed to be is shattered, and the image of what life is really about comes into sharp focus. There is no way to sugarcoat this one, but trust me, it can be handled. There is much to be learned from any Tower moment one goes through.

REVERSED MEANING: Avoidance, delaying the inevitable, resisting change

XVII - THE STAR

Aquarius, healing, hope, recovery

MEANING: Blessedly after the Tower (page 61), we receive the Star. She brings healing, hope, and recovery. The Fool is about to get much-needed help. In the depiction, a naked woman (literally stripped of any artifice or place to hide) kneels, pouring out two jugs of water, one into a pool (intuitive abilities) and the other on the ground, splitting into five streams (the five earthly senses). One of her feet sits in the water to demonstrate her connection to the world of Spirit, to the Divine. The other foot rests on the ground, showing the connection to the earthly plane. This card represents the zodiac sign of Aquarius and is similar to the water-bearer imagery. There is one large star circled by seven smaller stars, representing the seven chakras. When these are balanced, there is harmony within the body and spirit. This card depicts an intercessor pouring nourishment and healing into the land, which represents the client.

INTERPRETATION: In a reading, this is an excellent card to receive if the querent is going through a tough time, especially if it falls within a Present or Future position. I have found this card to represent loved ones on the other side who act as guardian angels and who are intervening on the querent's behalf. This card can also represent guides. The Star represents a light at the end of the tunnel. Better days are coming! The querent will be entering a more quiet, peaceful, and calm time of life. Hope is returning. This is a moment to start putting hard situations in the past. If the sitter inquires about a new love, this is a positive card to receive. The relationship can be healing and nourishing for the sitter. As mentioned, the Star represents the sign of Aquarius. So, the sitter may have been born under that sign or is exhibiting some of the sign's attributes, such as intelligence, uniqueness, and progressiveness. This represents a magical moment in the client's life where dreams can be connections to the other side. Psychic senses can also be heightened. Inspiration can strike during this time. Life is starting fresh and new when this card appears in a spread. Although the client may have had a Tower moment (page 61) to get here, the destruction did leave fertile soil from which new growth can spring forth.

REVERSED MEANING: Disappointment, despair, feeling alone

XVIII - THE MOON

Pisces, intuition, authenticity, wildness

MEANING: Time to let out a guttural howl! Strip away all that does not represent the true you, and let it bathe in the moonlight. The Fool can tap into his most authentic self with the aid of this card. In the Death card (page 55), you caught a sneak peek at this scene in the distance. The Death card does represent change, and the Moon completes the transformation. So, what was begun there will be finished here. The moon looms large in the background between two towers. It symbolizes intuition, sensitivity, and the unconscious. There sits a dog and a wolf separated by a thin path, representing the two sides of a person's nature—the wild (more authentic) personality and the tame (more cultivated) personality. In the light of the moon, hidden things come to the surface. Those parts of ourselves that we try to hide away from everyone else can come to the forefront. There's no better representation of this than someone who is a regular person by day but a snarling werewolf by full moon. The question is which one is the person's true form. In the foreground, arising from the water, is a crayfish that is just setting out on his journey of enlightenment and authenticity. The pool from which he emerges represents the subconscious and intuitive portals.

INTERPRETATION: In a reading, this card may indicate that things are not as they appear. Based on where the card falls in the spread, the querent may need to be advised that someone is hiding something from her. Alternatively, she may be hiding her true self from the rest of the world. Maybe there is a side to the querent that she is not quite ready to share. The Moon gives practical advice: stop worrying about what others think and simply be yourself. So what if people misunderstand you? That is their problem to work out, not yours. The Moon does represent the zodiac sign of Pisces. If the sitter herself is not born under that sign, someone she is asking about may be or the situation she finds herself in may have some Pisces qualities, such as illusory, dreamy, and emotional. Pisces are also known to be natural psychics. So, the sitter may feel tapped into her intuition when this card is pulled. This could also be a gentle nudge to the sitter that it is perfectly okay to embrace her wild side a little bit more. No one has ever suffered as a result of getting more in touch with themselves.

REVERSED MEANING: Enlightenment, truth revealed, resolution

XIX - THE SUN

Energized, success, joy

MEANING: This card is a positive one indeed. The Fool is emerging from a shadowy Moon phase (page 65) into a vibrant new day. Whatever fears have been lingering are now being evaporated by the searing light of the sun. This card is one of the rare few that does not have a negative connotation to it. And what's not to love? One half of the card is taken over by the warm, shining, golden sun. Beneath it stand four strong and beautiful sunflowers, soaking up its rays and representing the four suits of the Minor Arcana (Wands, Swords, Cups, Pentacles, page 76). The Sun blesses everyone equally. Beyond that, a naked babe carrying a red banner of passion rides a pure white stallion. Both the baby and horse represent purity, innocence, and joy. There is nothing to hide behind here. This is one's true authenticity shining through. There is also a sense of renewal with this card, since there is a baby being used to represent the querent instead of an adult. The energy is fresh and new and hopeful.

INTERPRETATION: In a reading, if a simple yes or no question is asked, the answer is easily yes. In fact, whatever the querent may be asking about is likely to have a positive outcome. Depending on the location in the spread, such as Present or Future, the client can be looking at an upcoming fabulous vacation or moving or traveling to a warm climate. This card can portend a simple beach trip. The client may be going through a childlike phase in life, such as starting out in a brand-new vocation or living in a different country. When I see this card in the Future position of a spread, I know that good times are ahead for the client. When it falls in the Present position, things are good currently. However, if the card appears in the Past position, and the cards in the Present and Future positions are somewhat negative, such as the Tower (page 61) or Devil (page 59), then unfortunately I know that the sitter is moving away from happier times into a rougher period. So, the card itself is not negative, but the position within the spread can affect the overall tone of the message.

REVERSED MEANING: Sadness, missed opportunity, depleted

XX - JUDGEMENT

Rebirth, calling, purpose, awakening

MEANING: Only a couple of steps away from the end of his journey, it is time for the Fool to be called forth to his true purpose. The Judgement card depicts the archangel Gabriel (Messenger of God) blowing his trumpet to call forth dead men, women, and children from their graves. Their arms are outstretched, ready to be judged and fully accept their fates. Rebirth is the main theme of this card. A mountain range looms in the background, making escape from the impending event impossible. Thankfully, this card is not to be taken literally as the Judgment Day prophesized in the Bible. This card is all about being called, but much more metaphorically. What is your true purpose or calling in this life? There is no more running from it. It is time to stand, face it, and accept it. As someone realizes a calling in their life, they have to make a decision about whether to follow through on it or not. That is what is at stake with this card.

INTERPRETATION: In a reading, this card likes to call the sitter on the carpet. This card is not about others judging the querent but rather about the querent judging herself too harshly. When this card is pulled, it is a time to assess whether how the querent is living is how she wants to be living. This can refer to a spiritual awakening for the sitter. It can also represent the sitter realizing that she has a role to play in this world and now truly knows what it is. Many spiritual leaders, psychics, and mediums tend to pull this card right before stepping into their roles. This card alludes to someone's purpose being that of service to others—a humanitarian. The imagery of this card can also relate to someone realizing that they are not marching to the beat of their own drum but to someone else's or society's at large. Based on where it falls within a spread, this card can indicate that the sitter is currently having this awakening or will be soon. This is also a reminder to the client that she should recognize her own goodness. Sometimes we are our own worst critic, and pulling this card can be a gentle way to remind the client that she needs to take a break from being too critical of herself.

REVERSED MEANING: Lying to yourself, criticism, failure to learn the lesson

XXI - THE WORLD

Success, completion, wholeness

MEANING: You made it! You have finally reached your destination. Success is at hand! The Fool has taken the final step on his journey and is feeling a sense of completion. Captured within the center of the World card is a naked woman draped in a purple cloth. In each hand she carries a wand, similar to the one the Magician (page 31) held aloft. This symbolizes that, what the Magician started, the World has now seen made manifest. She stands surrounded by a large laurel wreath, symbolizing triumph and completion. A laurel wreath can still be seen today in some countries as an emblem on master's degrees, denoting a high achievement. Within the corners of the card are the symbols of the four fixed signs of the zodiac—Aquarius (angel), Scorpio (eagle), Leo (lion), and Taurus (bull)—which are also seen in Wheel of Fortune (page 49). Both of these cards speak to the ebbs and flows of life, the cycles that we all go through. Note the background's blue color. Nothing is more uplifting than a crystal-clear blue sky, signifying that as one journey ends another one will soon take its place, and there is not a cloud in sight.

INTERPRETATION: In a reading, this is one of the most positive cards to pull. There is reason for the client to celebrate. Dreams coming true are right around the corner when this card pops up. After a hard-fought battle, success is near. This is the culmination of a lot of hard work, perseverance, and bravery. If the client asks a yes/no question, the answer is undoubtedly yes. This card also signals the end of one cycle and the brief pause before the beginning of the next. It is a great time for the client to take a moment to relish in her accomplishments. This card can signal a long-term project coming together, a promotion, a big move, or even stardom. The world is at the sitter's feet. If the sitter has been working on manifesting, this is a clear indication that she will soon see those intentions made real. There could be a situation that has come full circle for the querent as well. However, if there are still some final pieces the querent needs to work out, the World card also serves to point her toward the finish line. This is a big push from the Universe to say, "You're almost there, don't stop now!" Regardless of the situation at hand, the World card is one of positivity, where reflection of a job well done and looking ahead toward the next challenge go hand-in-hand.

REVERSED MEANING: Incomplete, success delayed, shortsighted

CHAPTER FOUR

THE MINOR ARCANA

THE BULK OF the tarot falls into the Minor Arcana, the fifty-six cards dealing with life's more common and routine occurrences. While the Major Arcana does illustrate those expanding and contracting moments of life, most of our day-to-day deals with the issues represented in the Minor Arcana. The situations found within the Major Arcana have long-term effects on the client. However, the situations within the Minor Arcana are of a more temporary nature. For example, the Minor Arcana can cover anything from getting a great idea to having a bad day at work. Although these events may be transitory, they are the still, quiet moments that shape our lives. For that reason, the Minor Arcana is special in its own right within the tarot. Simply put, you cannot have the Major Arcana without the Minor Arcana and vice versa.

When there is a majority of Minor Arcana cards found in a spread, the sitter is dealing with the day-in and day-out routines of life. The moment is not as urgent, and there are no major events taking place. The subject matter is not as deep as the Major Arcana, but whatever Major Arcana cards appear alongside the Minor Arcana in a reading can give more context to the bigger life lesson these smaller moments are contributing to. If most of the Minor Arcana cards in a spread are reversed, the sitter may be disconnected from her normal routine and needs to take a moment to reassess her current situation. The Minor Arcana is divided into four suits: Wands, Swords, Cups, and Pentacles.

✦ The **SUIT OF WANDS** is associated with the element of fire and represents passion, vitality, and movement. These cards show up in a reading about taking swift action and following your gut instinct. The Wands are also known as Rods, Staves, or Staffs in other decks.

✦ The **SUIT OF SWORDS** is associated with the element of air and represents intellect, thought processes, and know-how. These cards show up in a reading about decision-making and communicating. The Swords are also known as Daggers, Blades, and Knives in other decks.

✦ The **SUIT OF CUPS** is associated with the element of water and represents emotions, spirituality, and intuition. These cards show up in a reading about relationships and connection. The Cups are also known as Chalices or Goblets in other decks.

✦ The **SUIT OF PENTACLES** is associated with the element of earth and represents nature, finances, and work. These cards show up in a reading about achieving goals through effort. The Pentacles are also known as Coins, Discs, and Disks in other decks.

Pay attention when there is a majority of one suit found within a reading. When this is the case, the overall meaning of that suit is playing a major factor in the sitter's life. For example, if most of the cards drawn in a spread are Pentacles, it is safe to assume the sitter has a lot going on with money.

Within each suit, the cards begin with the ace and end with the king. The aces, regardless of suit, mark the beginning of the suit's journey. The **twos** represent balance and choices. The **threes** revolve around movement. The **fours** are about stability. The **fives** are the midpoint and normally offer a little uncertainty, as most halfway finished journeys do. The **sixes** talk of harmony or adjustment. The **sevens** speak to reevaluation. The **eights** are about change. The **nines** deal with fortitude. Lastly, the **tens** represent the completion of the journey and bring the suit full circle. When a certain number appears several times within a reading, take notice as the themes of that number are especially important. For example, if there are three fives found in a spread, the client is most likely dealing with a lot of chaotic energy at the moment.

Each suit has four **court cards**, which represent the sitter or other people in her life and are comprised of the page, knight, queen, and king. These can be friends, family members, lovers, enemies, coworkers, bosses, or old high school teachers. In a nutshell, anybody and everybody that you come into contact with can be represented by a court card. The court cards can represent anyone, regardless of age, sex, gender, race, or ethnicity. These cards, while representing individuals, also embody the energy of the ace through ten before it. The pages will always be full of energy and exuberance, and by the time the status of king is reached, decisions and movements have become more purposeful and planned.

The **pages**, while youthful in spirit, do not necessarily have to represent a person young in age. Traditionally, they represent someone who has a little maturing to do but also still has a zest for life. The **knights** are always ready to head off toward the horizon. If the pages represent mulling over an exciting thought, then the knights are ready to act on it. The **queens** have taken that youthful and action-oriented energy and combined it with life experience, making them wise and in tune with what's going on in their world. The **kings** represent the penultimate status in life, in which one can still remember the heady days of youth while incorporating the wisdom of lived experience.

In this book, we begin with the suit of Wands, as they represent the youthful energy of the tarot. Moving forward, we cover the Swords, the Cups, and finish with the Pentacles, the eldest sibling of the deck. Each suit symbolizes the four elements of fire, air, water, and earth—and their corresponding zodiac signs. Each suit represents a different season and offers timing in terms of days, months, weeks, and years. Again, the descriptions in this section are based on the Rider-Waite Tarot Deck and their cards are reproduced, but the meanings and interpretations can be used within any tarot deck you choose. For the ace through ten, beyond the meanings and interpretations, I include at least three cards that can strengthen or weaken that card's meaning. For the court cards, there are no strengthening or weakening cards, as the court cards represent actual people. However, there will be three celebrity examples given to help you grasp the basic personality of each court card. Also, while the court cards are predominantly representative of people within the sitter's life, at times these cards can represent situations. In that case, apply the overall attributes of the court card to the situation in order to decipher its meaning. Using this method can also give you an idea of what advice to give the sitter, as the court card's characteristics can be utilized to solve the issue at hand.

✦ THE SUIT OF WANDS ✦
Fire Energy / Spring / Days

The Wands are the passionate, energetic young bucks of the tarot. They inhabit the youthful exuberance of those ready to dash off and chase dreams, consequences be damned. It's an energy we should all tap into from time to time. The Wands represent the fire signs of the zodiac: Aries, Leo, and Sagittarius. Think of this suit as the starting point of life. This suit is heavily action oriented. These are the doers and the makers. This suit represents the season of spring. Just as the world begins to awaken, so too do the Wands. When calculating timing of an event, if the card pulled is a Wand, the time frame should occur within a matter of days.

ACE OF WANDS

Budding passion, new opportunity, flash of inspiration

MEANING: A seeming hand from the Universe reaches out to bring you an exciting offer. It is time to get those fires burning! A new

passion is being stoked within you. Maybe you're surfing through the TV channels and land on a late-night infomercial. Suddenly you feel inspired to come up with a hack that will make people's lives easier. The Ace of Wands captures that exact energy. It is the bolt of inspiration that strikes out of nowhere or the new hobby you absolutely fall in love with. This card is traditionally depicted as a wand sprouting budding leaves held aloft by a mystical

hand that has breached the thin veil between Heaven and Earth. The new buds on the wand represent potential passions springing forth. The hand represents the role Spirit plays in sending us opportunities that may not have been on our radar otherwise.

INTERPRETATION: In a reading, the Ace of Wands is a welcome sight. It signals fresh, new energy coming into the sitter's life. It's the buzz of a passion project first bubbling in your brain. The Wands are all about fiery, intense energy. However, they are not big on long-term planning. So, it is no surprise that the ace of this suit is ready to rev things up without much thought about the consequences. The question then becomes, will the sitter take this opportunity and run with it? And should she? If the card is surrounded by others that strengthen it, then the answer is an easy yes. But if the Ace of Wands is stymied by cards that weaken it, the client may want to take a pause before chasing this desire. This card is also good for a querent who has felt stuck and stagnant within her life. It's as if the Ace of Wands wanders into a listless room and yells, "Let's fire this party up!" Remember that the Wands represent the youthful feel of the tarot. They are all about exuberance, excitement, and energy. The Ace of Wands can represent the sitter starting a new hobby or passion project or an inspired feeling to be creative in many different forms.

STRENGTHENED BY: The Magician, the Fool, Knight of Wands
WEAKENED BY: The Hanged Man, Five of Pentacles, Four of Swords
REVERSED MEANING: Delay, creative block, inaction

TWO OF WANDS

Weighing options, assessing, making decisions

MEANING: That spark of inspiration felt in the Ace of Wands (page 79) may need some time to marinate. On the card, a person stands gazing out at the horizon, left hand clutching a wand while the

right holds a globe. It represents all the potential before you. A second wand sits propped up alone, representing another option to take. The person mulls over the possibilities from comfortable surroundings. There is safety in staying where you are, but there may be an adventure you're missing out on if you don't take a risk and travel outside of your comfort zone. The passions stirred deep within, while tempting to move ahead with, need a plan of action first.

This card represents a choice to be made. Do you play it safe or take a chance? No movement can come unless a decision is made either way. Take a reasonable amount of time to think on it, but eventually there will be a need to get moving. Is it time to take this passion to the next level or allow it to fizzle out?

INTERPRETATION: The sitter may have a burning desire to do something, but she feels unsure of how to go about it. The initial buzz has worn off a little, and now reality is sinking in. Yes, this bright, shiny object may hold so much potential for greatness. Then again, it could result in the querent's downfall. When the Two of Wands appears, clients are often at a crossroads. They may feel unsure of which way to go. However, nothing in life happens without decision-making. If there are surrounding cards that encourage the sitter to go for it, then the advice would be to chase that dream. However, if there are cards surrounding the Two of Wands that weaken it, caution should be considered. The timing may not be right for this project. Remember, a dream deferred is not a dream denied. This can also indicate that someone could be coming on board to help the client with her passion project. Another person may see the potential in this dream and be a willing participant in making it come true. The Two of Wands can also point to possible upcoming travel for the sitter.

STRENGTHENED BY: The Chariot, Two of Pentacles, Page of Pentacles
WEAKENED BY: The Hermit, the Devil, Eight of Swords
REVERSED MEANING: Indecision, frozen, overwhelmed

THREE OF WANDS

Looking ahead, forward momentum, plans underway
MEANING: So, it looks like a decision has been made. You're well on your way now! Sometimes when we get started on a path, nerves kick in and we start to doubt ourselves. We might want to double back and retrace our steps. But there's no need for that now. There is forward momentum to keep pushing ahead. In the Three of Wands, we see a person surveying new territory. We can tell many steps have been taken since the Two of Wands (page 80). The right hand now grasps the most forward wand while the left is unseen. Two more wands sit firmly rooted within the ground. Three ships pass by, signifying movement and action. What we have here is someone taking a little breather before continuing on with the journey ahead. This is all about finding

perspective and having some idea of what obstacles and goals are coming next.

INTERPRETATION: When the Three of Wands is pulled, the querent is on a journey. She may be wondering why she ever started it, but she is on one nonetheless. Anyone can relate to getting a spark of inspiration, making the choice to follow it, and then hitting a brick wall of fear and what-ifs. When this card pop ups, I know the sitter is going through the same situation. This card frequently comes up when a client asks whether she is on the right path in her life. Of course, the entire spread has to be taken into consideration, but if this card appears alongside cards that strengthen it, I would advise that she is indeed heading in the right direction. However, if cards that weaken the Three of Wands also show up, I may advise that

it is time to rethink her strategy. Maybe another course of action would be best. Many times, sitters pull this card when they are in need of a little reassurance and nothing more. Because the querent has gotten further in her journey, new opportunities are also possible for her. It is important to understand that, just as the Ace of Wands (page 79) requires bravery to chase that initial spark of inspiration, so too does the Three of Wands. Now is not the time to grow content. Most of the best opportunities for love, money, or health lie just beyond our comfort zones. So, this card also emphasizes being flexible and bold when striving toward your goals.

STRENGTHENED BY: The Empress, Strength, Seven of Wands
WEAKENED BY: Death, the Tower, the Hanged Man
REVERSED MEANING: Plans delayed, taking a different route, start over

FOUR OF WANDS

Celebrations, relaxation, stability

MEANING: Where's my party people? Put your hands in the air and wave 'em like you just don't care. Have you guessed what this card may be about? That's right—celebration! The journey of the Wands so far has been getting a spark of inspi-  ration, making the choice to follow it, and then pursuing the passion. Now, the Four of Wands arrives to celebrate a milestone met and enjoy a little break along the journey. Traditionally, the Four of Wands depicts a merry scene where two people in the background hold flower bouquets high in the air. Other partygoers mingle further back. In the foreground, a festive bough is held aloft by four wands. Four represents stability. Chairs have four legs. Tables have four legs. A room has four walls. You get the picture. Four is the foundation for a stable structure. Four represents the cardinal directions of north, south, east, and west and the natural elements of air, fire, water, and earth. This part of the path is where the passion of the Three of Wands (page 81) finds balance. You're finally starting to hit your groove. Others have begun to notice not only the change in you but also your accomplishments while you have been chasing your dream. Take time to revel in this moment!

INTERPRETATION: When the Four of Wands is pulled, the querent is sure to be celebrating soon. This card can represent an upcoming wedding, birthday, anniversary, or graduation. It could represent a big party. The client may be the one hosting it, or it could be thrown on her behalf. This card can also point to a reunion or homecoming. The road has probably been a little rocky for the sitter lately. It is not necessarily easy work chasing a dream. But the Four of Wands finally offers that first sigh of relief. It is the validation so deeply needed to continue on the journey. For example, a high school or college graduation marks the completion of one stage of life and affirms the choices made along the way. However, it is not the end of pursuing a passion. There are next steps to be taken, such as securing a job or receiving more education. Still, the achievement should be acknowledged, and a pause should be taken before continuing down the road of life.

STRENGTHENED BY: The Lovers, Six of Wands, Three of Cups
WEAKENED BY: The Tower, the Hermit, Seven of Swords
REVERSED MEANING: Canceled event, bad marriage, social anxiety

FIVE OF WANDS

Strife, arguments, chaotic situation

MEANING: So, okay. One card ago there were parties and celebrations being thrown in your honor. And now? Everyone's fighting.

As you may have already realized, once you reach a modicum of success in life, others love to come out of the woodwork and put in their two cents. How did you manage to get to this point without their sage advice? (Insert eye roll here.) People may be well intentioned with their unsolicited input, but that does not mean it's not frustrating and often not that helpful. Depicted on the Five of Wands are five separate individuals, each carrying a rather long wand, seemingly in the midst of a battle. However, upon closer inspection, none of the wands are hitting anyone. Rather, they represent the passionate position each individual person is trying to explain to the other, resulting in a chaotic scene. Fives are rather notorious within numerology and tarot. It is the odd-numbered step between four and six that lacks either's stability. Things run a little hinky at this level.

INTERPRETATION: When this card is pulled, things are not as peaceful as the querent would like. She most likely finds herself in the middle of a chaotic scene. For example, she may find that a trusted friend and confidant has suddenly become a direct competitor. While it is nice to know that pursuing a goal can inspire others, watching a friend choose competition over support can be disappointing. This card can also represent a business partnership hitting a bumpy patch. The Five of Wands represents superficial arguments within a family or friend group as well. What is needed in this situation is for someone to realize the cause of the conflict isn't that deep. This is truly one of those situations where, although the sitter may be right, she needs to weigh the cost of losing a relationship with a trusted colleague, friend, or family member. If this card is pulled with other cards that strengthen its meaning of discord, this fight unfortunately may cause long-standing damage. However, if it is surrounded by cards that weaken its meaning and reinforce teamwork and cooler heads prevailing, this is a passing argument that everyone involved will probably look back on in time and laugh.

STRENGTHENED BY: The Tower, Five of Swords, Seven of Wands
WEAKENED BY: Three of Cups, Three of Pentacles, Four of Swords
REVERSED MEANING: Harmony, peace, cooler heads prevail

SIX OF WANDS

Victory, triumph, promotion

MEANING: Of course, you would never gloat, but maybe you were the voice of reason and won out in the Five of Wands (page 84). Here you sit now with a wreath of victory held high and your friends and family lauding you for your kind eyes and biting intellect. Okay, so maybe the last part is taking some poetic license. But it does paint a picture, right? In this card a rider, crowned with a laurel wreath, comes in on a horse decked out in full regalia.

Others can be seen in the ba   id walking alongside, cheering
the rider on. All the surro   noopla seems to be centered on
the rider. The white hor   sents purity and perseverance. The
rider is draped in a re   , with red representing passion. The
rider has not h   ᵣ   ᵤon a parade by chance. The celebration
occurs becaᵧ   ᵣder's actions, and there is pride to be had
in hard ᵥ   off.

I   ᴛɪᴏɴ: When this card appears in a reading, a milestone
        n reached by the client or soon will be, depending on where
    ᴎe spread the card lands. This is an accomplishment the client
takes a lot of pride in. This can take the form of anything from

 a pat on the back at work to a promotion or
raise. The Six of Wands also indicates that this
is not only an achievement for the querent but
also one that others acknowledge and for which
they show pride for the querent. So, it can also
represent an award won, a community recognition, a business expansion, or a growing social
media presence. Again, because it is within the
Wands suit, these achievements are based on
following one's passions. This could be a hobby
that turns into a career or a wild dream that inspires the sitter to
change her life. And while this milestone is special, it is also not
the end of the journey. There is still more road to travel. If this card
falls within the Outcome position, indicating it has yet to happen
and the client seems confused as to why she would be reaching a
milestone, it can be a gentle reminder from Spirit to remain persistent in her pursuits because the payoff is coming.

STRENGTHENED BY: The Chariot, the World, Four of Wands
WEAKENED BY: The Devil, Seven of Swords, Eight of Swords
REVERSED MEANING: Defeat, a fall from grace, empty victory

SEVEN OF WANDS

Defending yourself, perseverance, determination

MEANING: A person stands on a hill, wand in hand in a defensive stance. A few feet below, six wands stretch up in an attack. The

person has on two different shoes, illustrating this fight may not have been anticipated. Oh no, what's happening now? While we may not want to admit it, sometimes others' good news can cause the stirrings of the green-eyed monster in us all. Remember, the Wands represent passion. Passions and tempers flare. Once someone has followed a good idea and transformed it, such as into a good business or online offering or successful social media plat-

form, competitors become acutely aware. Ideally, we should realize that there is more than enough to go around and that everyone should bolster and support each other, but we humans fall short of the ideal. As you may have realized by now, the suit of Wands is a bit of a roller coaster. Such is life. One day, you're on top of the world, celebrated for your great successes, and the next you may feel like everyone's out to get you. The Seven of Wands tends to feel more like the latter.

INTERPRETATION: All right, there are wolves at the door. What should clients do about it? Open the door and let them in? Or stand and defend themselves? When this card is pulled, it is time for the client to stand her ground. In regards to business/career matters, the sitter may be facing stiff competition. Someone may have opened a shop next door, replicating her business model. There may be several more people online offering the same services that she does. The question is, does she give up or does she distinguish herself from the competition and hold on to the progress she has made? In terms of love, this card can represent a relationship that has begun to feel like a battlefield. One or both partners tend to want to justify themselves in arguments. While this card, regardless of the situation, seems to be full of fights and defensive posturing, ultimately the sitter should come out on top. If a question is asked about whether something is worth fighting for or continuing to pursue, the answer is yes, but only if the sitter is willing to put in the work and stay persistent when the road gets rough.

STRENGTHENED BY: Strength, Five of Swords, Five of Wands
WEAKENED BY: The Hermit, Wheel of Fortune, Four of Cups
REVERSED MEANING: Giving up, ineffective, losing heart

EIGHT OF WANDS

Incoming news, busy time, movement

MEANING: Whew, yet another obstacle overcome! Now that the would-be troublemakers have been dealt with in the Seven of Wands (page 87), the Eight of Wands is ready

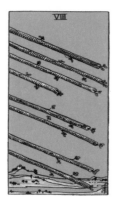

to get back to work. And there is plenty to go around. Actually, there is so much going on at this point in the journey of the suit of Wands that no one appears on the card itself. There are eight wands, speeding through the air. The sky is sparkling blue without a cloud in sight. This indicates there is nothing stopping this action from occurring. The landscape below features a beautiful wide river, giving sustenance to the green hills around it. Things are rolling right along and looking good while they do.

INTERPRETATION: When this card is pulled, the querent is sure to receive some news, and fast! The momentum in her life has been building, and now it will explode into action. The Eight of Wands indicates that things are about to get busy. This is the part of every dream where the real work is done to make it come true. This is the burning the midnight oil card, the rise and grind card, the digging deep and going for it card. There is a tendency for someone to almost become obsessive about chasing a goal when this card appears. It is best to advise the client that, while hard work does pay off, there should always be some time left to rest and relax so there is a balance. The Eight of Wands indicates that since the earlier obstacles of outside people and situations have been sorted the road is open to get a lot of things done. This is when someone gets into the zone and a lot of work gets done. The best way to handle the energy of this card is to get in the flow. That means to be flexible with plans and, as opportunities arise, go with them instead of working against them. The sitter may also be struck by a brand-new idea when this card is pulled. While that bright, shiny new object may be tempting to follow, it is best to hone in on the current project at hand. The sitter can always keep the newly found inspiration in her back pocket to pull out once this project is completed.

STRENGTHENED BY: The Chariot, Six of Swords, Knight of Swords
WEAKENED BY: The Hanged Man, Temperance, Four of Swords
REVERSED MEANING: No change, no news, stagnant

NINE OF WANDS

Nearly there, resilience, last stand

MEANING: Maybe you're noticing a trend with the suit of Wands. It contains an alternating pattern between super-high highs and super-low lows. Aren't passions much the same? So, consider this card the last stand in the battle before reaching your passionate goals. This card depicts a person standing, head bandaged and eyes wary of the eight wands all around. The obviously tired and weary individual leans on the ninth wand. There seems to be a real conflict going on in the person's mind. You can almost see the internal calculations, determining whether all of this hard work is even worth it. More times than not, the conclusion reached is that there is still some fight left in the old girl.

INTERPRETATION: When this card is pulled, my first thought always is, "Don't quit!" I know when I see this card for a client that she has been through it. She most likely feels exhausted, emotionally and physically, because she has been fighting, battling, and working so hard to reach her goals. I love when sitters get a reading and this card comes out. I know it's Spirit's way of sending them a pep talk. This card represents that moment in life when the finish line is in sight but the querent is not sure if she has enough energy to make it there. The great news here: this card shows she does. It is

perfectly okay to take a small break or reassess priorities when this card pops up. However, the advice is to make sure to get back up once rested. The client is too close to give up now. When this card comes up, the querent is also being given an opportunity to reassess her goals and to remember why she started down this path in the first place. In a love reading, this could be a chance for the client to think back on why she wants to stay in a relationship. Though things may have been rocky, there may be enough to salvage if both partners agree to work on it. I see this card come up quite a bit when someone is considering a divorce. If the couple has yet to consider counseling, I recommend it, as working through issues and finding that initial spark is always possible.

STRENGTHENED BY: Strength, the Star, Four of Swords
WEAKENED BY: The Tower, Five of Pentacles, Eight of Cups
REVERSED MEANING: Giving in, secret enemy, broken spirit

TEN OF WANDS

Overwhelmed, need to streamline, end of cycle

MEANING: Finally! The end of this hard cycle is here! There have been many ups and downs. Your passions have turned you this way and that. Maybe what started out as a cute idea about making stickers of funny memes has now grown into a behemoth of international proportions. Or it could be that you're moved from relative obscurity into a well-known social media star. In either example, it is clear that the suit of Wands takes us on quite the ride. Now, in the Ten of Wands, there is some completion to look forward to. In the card, a person is bent over, carrying a large bundle of ten wands. It

seems to be a physically taxing chore. A small town is in the distance, not too far away. The person seems resolute on finishing this task, taking confident strides. While the work does seem to be hard, the bounty is also great. These ten wands can benefit many different people. All this hard work will pay off.

INTERPRETATION: This card can take on a few different meanings. Tens are known for completion. It is the end of a cycle. This will be welcome news to the sitter if things have been hard for a long time. Pulling this card indicates that the client has reached the end of this particular pursuit of passion. Things feel overwhelming. If this card is pulled in a business/career reading, the sitter feels burned out! She is most likely dealing with being overworked and underappreciated. She may be considering quitting her job. In a love reading, the burdens of this particular relationship may be too much to bear. This is also a card of consideration. It may not necessarily be that the sitter is overworked but rather she has too many irons in the fire. This is an indication to pare down. The sitter needs to be selective about which and how many passions she needs to continue to chase. When someone is being pulled in too many different directions, even those projects that used to stoke the fires of the sitter's heart may now feel like an anchor weighing her down. I normally advise a client that it is more than okay to take some time to listen to that inner guidance regarding the next step.

STRENGTHENED BY: Death, Ten of Swords, Eight of Cups
WEAKENED BY: The Sun, Ace of Wands, Page of Pentacles
REVERSED MEANING: Not releasing burdens, relinquishing power, giving up too soon

COURT CARDS
Aries, Leo, Sagittarius

Within the suit of Wands, the court cards represent the fire signs of Aries, Leo, and Sagittarius. These individuals are full of fire power and passionate pursuits. They are go-getters, leaders, and fire-brands. If you're having a party, you want a fire sign there to liven it up. If you're heading off to war, you will want a fire sign by your side. These people, regardless of biological age, will always have a young, fresh energy and love to experience everything life has to offer. Sometimes, they are a little too eager to take off on an adventure, rather than thinking it through, so these court cards can run into a few issues. But they are never down for long.

PAGE OF WANDS
Enthusiastic, curious, up for anything
MEANING: Your mama probably warned you about a Page of Wands because this fire sign is feisty, frisky, and fearless. In this card the Page of Wands stands admiring a wand sprouting with new buds. This young page is dressed in a dapper tunic covered in salamanders, which represent rebirth, passion, and the ability to withstand fire, a perfect representation for this individual. The page's feet are

firmly planted on the ground. There is no movement indicated within the scene depicted. So, while this person may be bubbling with ideas and inspiration, a full plan of action has yet to come together. The background is a desert, indicating that this type of person has the resilience and determination to birth new ideas even in seemingly barren land. It also points to the fact that this individual may not always weigh out every decision before setting off on a journey. Three celebrities that encapsulate this young page's energy are Sadie Sink, Max from *Stranger Things* (Aries), Marsai

PAGE of WANDS.

Martin (Leo), and Hailee Steinfeld (Sagittarius). All three share that fire energy, which make them natural risk-takers who benefit big time from taking a leap of faith.

INTERPRETATION: The Page of Wands is a little ball of fire, waiting for a place to explode . . . in a good way. The person this card represents is full of life and ready for adventure. This person can be an Aries, Leo, or Sagittarius; sun, moon, or rising sign; or at the very least exhibit the characteristics of the fire signs. The person doesn't necessarily have to be young in years but may be youthful in personality or in their approach to life. Depending on the spread and where the card lands within it, the Page of Wands either represents the sitter herself or someone she is inquiring about. This can also explain a situation at hand and that the best approach to take would be going after it with all the client's got. There is a youthful exuberance and optimism to this card that can be utilized to work in the client's favor. Depending on surrounding cards, such as the Hanged Man (page 53) or the Devil (page 59), it may be best to caution the client to take a more measured approach or take a moment to think about what she is about to embark on, as rushing in headfirst may be a little too risky at the moment. On the other hand, if this card appears with the Magician (page 31) or the Six of Wands (page 85), it may be best to throw caution to the wind and embrace a naïve, devil-may-care attitude about the situation.

REVERSED MEANING: Closed off, immature, delayed message

KNIGHT OF WANDS

Charming, pushing forward, adventurous

MEANING: Okay, so the Knight of Wands is like the older sibling who takes the Page of Wands's idea and runs with it. Literally. While the page is still noodling over a bright shiny idea, the knight, without much planning beforehand, heads right into the fray.

Within the card, the knight sits atop a horse, rearing up on its hind legs, ready to run. The knight holds the reins in one hand while holding the wand upright in the other. Again, like the younger page, the knight also wears a tunic decorated in salamanders to symbolize the passion and fiery nature within. In the background is a desert scene, indicating that tough terrains or vast wilderness are no match for the passionate determination of the Knight of Wands.

KNIGHT of WANDS

Three celebrities that channel the Knight of Wands's energy are Chance the Rapper (Aries), Bill Skarsgård (Leo), and Zoë Kravitz (Sagittarius). These forward-thinking and boundary-pushing artists have the guts and gusto to follow their biggest dreams and reach them!

INTERPRETATION: When this card comes up and it is determined to represent the client herself (due to the spread used and where the card falls within it), I know that she is a firecracker who is a go-getter and someone who rarely takes no for an answer. The client may in fact be an Aries, Leo, or Sagittarius; sun, moon, or rising sign; or at least exhibit the attributes of a fire sign. When this card appears, the sitter is most likely raring to get started on a passion project, new job, or possible move to an entirely new city. Her enthusiasm and excitement about future events may even be infectious. I love when sitters are represented by this card because I know that not much will get in their way when chasing a dream. It's an exciting card to pull. When the card is more likely to represent the overall feel of a situation and/or how to deal with it, it is important to look to surrounding cards for what approach to take. If the Hanged Man (page 53) or the Hermit (page 47) appears with this card, the querent may want to slow down a little before continuing to run ahead. More information may be needed before heading down this path. With this card, it is sometimes hard to caution the querent to wait before starting out because she already has, but she may be able to make a U-turn and course correct before it is too late. However, if the Fool (page 29) or Ace of Wands (page 79) appears alongside this card, the wind is at the sitter's back, and she should get ready to fly.

REVERSED MEANING: Arrogance, brash, reckless

QUEEN OF WANDS

Vivacious, courageous, passionate

MEANING: She is beauty. She is grace. She will flip you off to your face. She is the Queen of Wands. This queen is confident, courageous, and capable. Sitting upon a throne flanked by two lions, this queen rules by the warmth of her heart and the fire in her veins. She holds her wand within her right hand and a giant sunflower in her left. At her feet sits a single black cat, representing not only her independent streak but also her ability to face her own inner demons. The yellow of her robes represents her upbeat personality and positive outlook. The sunflowers represent joy and fertility. The lions symbolize strength. The Queen of Wands takes all the exuberance and vitality of a youthful fire sign, wraps a well-weathered wisdom around it, and continues to the carry the torch of passions into the future. Think of your feisty friend who never backs

down from a fight and almost always lands on her feet. She is most likely to lead an activist charge or head up the newest committee at work. That is the energy of the Queen of Wands. Three celebrities who harness their fiery queen energy on a daily basis are Lady Gaga (Aries), Viola Davis (Leo), and Nicki Minaj (Sagittarius). Would you want to challenge Gaga to a sing off, try to upstage Viola, or rap battle against Nicki? Nah, me neither.

INTERPRETATION: When this fearsome card is pulled, I know that the client is a force to be reckoned with. She is someone who people gravitate toward and will probably always elect to lead them, from high school class president to union liaison at work. This individual knows how to get a job done. She is a delegator and a facilitator and a natural-born leader. It can be possible that this card represents someone else in the querent's life. If it is a love reading, this person can definitely bring intense passion into a relationship. This card pops up sometimes when a client has forgotten who she is. A bit of mojo may be lacking and the client might feel a little down on herself. If I see this card appear, I know that Spirit wants me to deliver the pep talk the client desperately needs. Most likely, whatever situation the sitter is facing can be overcome by remembering what a badass she is. Truly. The card can also represent what action should be taken regarding a situation. Whether it is about career, relationships, or health, the advice from the Queen of Wands is to forge ahead with passionate determination and fortitude.

REVERSED MEANING: Petty, jealous, spiteful

KING OF WANDS

Visionary, bold, direct

MEANING: The King of Wands is someone who is ruled by the same fire he uses to motivate others. He has vision, direction, and the boldness to acquire it all. At times, he can speak harshly, but he knows his own mind, and it is often difficult to get him off course once he has started something. When a person with King of Wands energy walks into the room, you know it. These individuals have a big presence and a larger-than-life persona. This card depicts the king sitting on his throne with fully mature wand in hand, growth evident throughout. The banner of the throne is yellow, covered in lions and salamanders. The yellow coloring is no accident. It was selected to represent passion. The lions and salamanders represent strength  and fire. The salamanders are eating their own tails, which alludes to infinity and the continuous cycle of life. Brian Tyree Henry (Aries), Chris Hemsworth (Leo), and Jay-Z (Sagittarius) epitomize the King of Wands vibe. These gentlemen are moguls, media mavens, and magnetic personalities, all indicative of their fiery foundation.

INTERPRETATION: When the King of Wands appears in a reading, things are about to get spicy. This person can be quite the dynamic romantic or energizing business partner. If it is determined that this card represents the querent herself, I would have no doubts in her ability to make all her dreams come true. People probably flock to her, due to her magnetism and ability to inspire others. If the King of Wands represents a love interest for the client, she should know this person can be passionate—but with fire comes the threat of burns. Depending on the client and the situation she finds herself in with this person, the relationship can burn too hot. If there are issues within the relationship, the fire may have turned into cool embers. When this card appears in a business reading, the sitter is ready to take the helm. If there is a question about whether the sitter is ready to lead or move up in the business world, this card should quell any of those doubts. This card is an absolute yes, you can! If the card falls in the "What Will Be" position of a reading, the advice is crystal clear. I advise my clients to step into their power and get ready to shine because it is their time to step up.

REVERSED MEANING: Bully, volatile, dishonest

✦ THE SUIT OF SWORDS ✦
Air Energy / Winter / Weeks

On to the heady suit of Swords! This suit is all about air energy and represents the zodiac signs of Gemini, Libra, and Aquarius that are characterized within the court cards. This is the intellectual suit of the tarot and represents being a little further down life's path. After all the fiery, impetuous energy of the Wands, the Swords come along to finally think about everything that's happened. This deals with mental processes, philosophical thoughts, analytical thinking, and the overall power of the mind. This suit represents the season of winter. When calculating timing of an event, if the card pulled is a Sword, the time frame should occur within a matter of weeks.

ACE OF SWORDS
Breakthrough, eureka, new idea
MEANING: A hand reaches out from the ether and implants a new idea into your mind. Eureka! You've got it! The mind is incredibly powerful, and the Ace of Swords is the first step on that journey through the world of thoughts, ideas, and intellect. Traditionally, this card depicts a hand holding a two-sided sword. The Ace of Swords represents a shiny new idea popping into your head or possibly a fresh way of seeing an old problem, which finally leads to its

resolution. A crown hovers at the tip of the sword to represent the success that will happen if this new idea is acted upon. However, there are mountains in the background. So, mental toughness will be required in order to meet these goals. Again, the mind is being represented by the sword. Just as a sword can wound, cut, and pierce, so too can your mind. If you're not careful, sometimes the mind's biggest victim is yourself.

INTERPRETATION: When this card appears in a reading, the client has probably already been struck with a great idea or is just about to be. This is a welcome sight if the client has felt stuck or unsure about which way to go in life. If it appears with cards dealing with money, such as the Ace of Pentacles (page 137) or Eight of Pentacles (page 144), this new idea can turn out to be lucrative for the sitter. In fact, it may be pointing to a real calling in the client's life. Because this ace is from the suit of Swords, the idea and/or project the sitter may want to begin will most likely be something requiring mental agility. The querent may have a great idea for a new podcast, want to take a class in speechmaking, or even write a book. Remember, communication skills require the use of mental processes. If the card represents the situation at hand based on the spread layout, it can refer to the need of the sitter to look at her current situation with new eyes. Maybe a different approach is warranted to produce different results. The Ace of Wands (page 79) can also appear quite frequently when the client has had or is about to have prophetic dreams, which can also lead to solutions to long-standing problems.

STRENGTHENED BY: The Magician, the Sun, Ace of Wands
WEAKENED BY: The Hanged Man, the Devil, Four of Swords
REVERSED MEANING: Nothing new coming, writer's block, frustration

TWO OF SWORDS

Confusion, uncertainty, difficult choices

MEANING: So, what happens right after you have an amazing idea that you felt totally secure about a few days ago? That's right! Crippling worry and doubt involving every little detail about it. It is that exact moment that is portrayed by the Two of Swords. A blindfolded person sits with crossed arms, each holding a sword. The swords are of equal length and shape. In the background is a vast body of water with scattered jagged rocks jutting to the surface. This indicates that the person is facing a difficult choice. Due to the equality of the two swords, both options feel equally valid and important. The blindfold tells us that the person either does not have enough information to make this decision or it is a case of self-imposed ignorance in order to keep from making a choice. The crescent moon hanging prominently in the sky points to the fact that although this is the suit of Swords, a reliance on both

intuition and intellect will be needed to sort out this situation.

INTERPRETATION: Ever heard the phrase, "Getting in your own way"? When this card appears, it truly embodies that statement. There are choices for the client to make, but she cannot seem to make one, mostly due to her own overanalyzing and/or complete lack of insight. This can come up when a client wants to change jobs. She does not have enough information about the new job to feel secure enough to leave the safety and stability of her current job. Should she go or should she stay? When pulling this card, it is always a good idea to pay attention to the card that is pulled directly next to it, as it can give some indication as to what the client needs to make a decision about or possibly what that decision needs to be. The important point to remember about the

Two of Swords is that ultimately a choice must be made. There are no perfect decisions. It should be advised that making no choice is still a choice, and it is much better to be in the driver's seat in life instead of the passenger's seat. This can also represent a sitter's low-key mental fog. There are times in life when we all fall victim to the blahs. Nothing too bad is happening, but neither is anything too exciting. Frequently the Two of Swords will appear if this is how the sitter has been feeling. Again, the surrounding cards can determine how to get out of it.

STRENGTHENED BY: The Hanged Man, Seven of Cups, Eight of Swords
WEAKENED BY: The High Priestess, Strength, Ace of Swords
REVERSED MEANING: Indecision, information comes to light, overconfident

THREE OF SWORDS
Heartbreak, betrayal, emotional release
MEANING: So, sometimes people we love, situations we're in, or choices we make do not turn out the way we had hoped. Life is not always easy or happy. There are going to be times that do not feel great. With the Three of Swords, this is one of those times. The card shows a simple illustration of a red heart pierced by three sharp swords. Of course, a sword to the heart is never a positive. These represent being wounded by someone's actions or words. Behind the heart are actively raining dark heavy clouds, representing emotional distress over the situation. It is not a pleasant picture. However, rain clouds come and go quite quickly. This is a reminder that hard times will not last forever. Perhaps that thought can dull the pain, if only a little.

INTERPRETATION: This is one of those tarot cards that no one likes to see pop up. Although it is in the suit of Swords, the pain felt is usually more than mental, extending into emotional and even physical wellness at times. If this reading is related to career or finances, the Three of Swords can indicate that a facet of that great idea or project is not going to work out. When things do not work out exactly as planned, there is often some upset. We tend to have a set picture in our minds of how things should go. When they don't, it is almost always a case of hurting our own feelings. This card also appears to let the client know that someone has misused her trust. Many times, the client is not aware of this betrayal, making it all the more difficult to bear. If this card falls within the Past position, the client may already be dealing with this painful realization, or if it falls in the Future position, she will have a

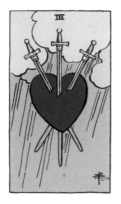

heads-up that it is coming. It is important to remind the client that she is allowed and, even more importantly, should express the emotions that come with this heartbreak. Sometimes this card can appear to remind the client that she needs to get in touch with the old hurts that she has been holding on to and let them go. There is still the journey of life to experience, and this intense pain cannot be used as an excuse for the sitter to give up on any projects

or passions. Obviously, this card can point to infidelity within a relationship; however, I find it is best to simply state that there has been a betrayal. Many times, clients ask whether a significant other is cheating. Revealing sensitive information is a heavy burden for a reader to bear. This card does not necessarily mean that the other person has been unfaithful, but there can be lying or deception that will lead to heartache for the client. Let the client determine for herself how far the betrayal goes. It is never a good idea to tell someone there is cheating happening only to find out there has not been.

STRENGTHENED BY: The Tower, Five of Cups, Eight of Cups

WEAKENED BY: The Lovers, the Sun, the World

REVERSED MEANING: Reconciliation, healing, lack of emotion

FOUR OF SWORDS

Rest, pause, reconsider

MEANING: Coming on the heels of the Three of Swords (page 101), in which our hearts have been bruised and our minds may be reeling, what better course of action to take than a little rest and relaxation? Sometimes, a simple pause or withdrawing from the world for a while is just what the doctor ordered. Traditionally, this card depicts a person lying above a tomb with one sword beneath them while the other three swords hang above their torso. The single sword represents a clear, direct focus for the person. The other three swords represent additional concerns and worries the person is struggling with. Again, the suit of Swords deals  with all things mental. How many times have you driven yourself a little batty by going over something again and again in your mind? All the worrying in the world will never change a situation, but try telling that to your brain at three o'clock in the morning, when you're obsessing over that one dumb thing you said in fifth grade.

INTERPRETATION: When this card appears, I know immediately that the client needs to take a break. Depending on the surrounding cards, this break may need to be from her job, her partner, or her worries. Perhaps there is a lot of arguing going on in her love life. This card's appearance would clearly indicate taking a pause. That does not necessarily mean breaking up with the person, but perhaps it suggests learning how to give each other space when things get too heated. Maybe the client has been too stressed with work.

When this card shows up, it is best to advise the client to look into her PTO and take a vacation. This is a subtle way Spirit lets sitters know that it would be best to heed their advice and take a much-needed rest now before bigger problems develop. This card also comes up to let the client know that she is about to hit the next level on her journey, and with milestones it is always best to rest up before moving on to the next challenge. This card can be thought of as a pit stop on the road to success. While you can throw on a Depends and drive nonstop from New York to Los Angeles in record time, the question is: Should you? Probably not, right? Let's pull that car on over and stretch your legs and use the facilities. You and your bladder will be glad you did.

STRENGTHENED BY: The Hermit, the Hanged Man, Nine of Wands
WEAKENED BY: The Chariot, the Sun, Knight of Swords
REVERSED MEANING: Becoming active, charging ahead, end of sabbatical

FIVE OF SWORDS

Pick your battles, arguments, conflict

MEANING: It is possible that, if the advice of the Four of Swords (page 103) was not heeded, then you have found yourself here, battling fate, others, and yourself. Again, fives contain unexpected energy. They are the midpoint through the journey of the Minor Arcana, and things tend to get a little rocky midway through any trip. Since the suit of Swords deals with mental processes, these fights are of a mental nature. If the battle is with oneself, this can encompass a racing mind, intrusive thoughts, and paranoia, as well as negative self-speak and a harsh inner critic. If the fight is with others, it can be reflected in biting words, nasty texts, and harsh phone calls. The Five of Swords does not traditionally indicate a physical altercation. The card itself shows the five swords split between three people. One carries off the majority of the swords, while two other individuals slump away, their swords on the ground. Clearly, someone has won while others have lost. But is it that black and white? The victor in this scenario may have won the battle but can still lose the war.

INTERPRETATION: When this card appears in a reading, I ask the client whether she has been dealing with some type of drama in her life. The answer is usually a resounding yes. If this card appears with the Nine of Swords (page 110) or the Hanged Man (page 53), the drama is more internal, where the client is struggling with her own mind. This can represent a depressive episode, high stress level, or unresolved trauma. As mentioned earlier, if a sitter seems to be in need of psychological or psychiatric help, remember to gently refer this option (page 24). Explain that you are not a trained  physician and sometimes the reading serves its purpose by advising the sitter to seek professional treatment. When the conflict is with other people, a question should be considered: Is winning at all costs an effective strategy? This can be as simple as wanting to win an argument because the querent just knows she is right or continuing a long-standing feud because, at this point, it is more about saving face than doing what is needed. Sometimes, this card can appear when a querent has been pushed to her limits by others and finally strikes back. It may be necessary at times to sever relationships if they are toxic and cross boundaries. Yes, there will be loss in those instances as well, but ultimately, it is better for the client's mental health.

STRENGTHENED BY: The Devil, Five of Wands, Ten of Swords
WEAKENED BY: Three of Cups, Three of Pentacles, Six of Wands
REVERSED MEANING: Resolution, vulnerability, avoiding conflict

SIX OF SWORDS

Moving away, travel, easier times ahead

MEANING: After the loss of the Five of Swords (page 104), it is often best to put some distance between yourself and the past. This can

be in the form of establishing boundaries with those who bring strife into your life or an actual physical move in which you have a fresh start to begin anew. Again, whether it is emotional or physical distancing, the relief from the stress will be mental. Traditionally, this card depicts a cloaked adult and child sitting in a boat while someone paddles for them. The move seems to be happening somewhat in secret. It is often best not to give problem people a heads-up before making a change. Also, the cloak is a way to signify that there may be a sadness to this move. There are six swords sticking into the boat, representing some of the old baggage following them into their future. On the right side of the boat, the water is churning and turbulent, but on the left the water is more serene and peaceful, indicating that better times lie ahead.

INTERPRETATION: This card is an easy yes if the client asks if she will be moving soon. When this card appears, it will happen. Depending on the full card spread, you may be able to determine when the move will occur. It is also a strong indicator that the client will be moving if this card appears alongside other tarot cards that strengthen it. This can also indicate that a new job can be on the horizon, one that may cause the sitter to move. Within a relationship, this can represent a separation. It can mean moving out if living together or giving each other space to work things out. The best way to handle strife is to put as much distance between it and yourself as possible. This should be stressed to the sitter if she is unsure about making a move or putting distance between herself and someone else. Spirit will always find the easiest and most straightforward way to give a sitter the message needed at that exact moment in her life. That is the intelligence of Spirit.

STRENGTHENED BY: The Chariot, Three of Wands, Eight of Wands
WEAKENED BY: The Hanged Man, Four of Swords, Ten of Wands
REVERSED MEANING: Stuck, travel plans canceled, troubled waters

SEVEN OF SWORDS

Lying, deception, cheating

MEANING: The suit of Swords likes to explore all the depths of the mental world. The Seven of Swords is no exception, as it deals

with our ability to lie to others and to ourselves. In this card, a person is seen making off with five swords with two swords left behind. A sly smile crosses the person's lips, and there is a sense of satisfaction by seemingly getting away with it. There are some tents in the background, and perhaps people were too busy to notice the person sneaking away, or maybe it was planned months in advance. Is the person stealing something or retrieving what is rightfully theirs? Maybe a little sneakiness is warranted due to the situation, but ultimately any time dishonesty is used there is a tendency to have it backfire on the person who uses it.

INTERPRETATION: When I see this card in a reading, I know someone somewhere in the client's life is a liar, liar pants on fire. All kidding aside, this card definitely points to deception. If this card appears alongside the Moon (page 65) or Seven of Cups (page 126), it is possible that the person lying to the client is herself. She may be well aware that something is not going right in her life, but there is a level of denial happening. She may be involved in some duplicitous behavior that she is not ready to own up to yet. If you haven't realized it yet, the tarot will definitely call you out on all your BS. It is a straightforward method of divination that is not intended to be insulting. It's a frank look into the sitter's life in order to be as helpful as possible. So, be gentle with the client when discussing this card. For example, the sitter may ask whether things will work out between her and her partner. If surrounding cards seem to imply that the answer is no, such as the Devil (page 59) or the Three of Swords (page 101), and the Seven of Swords represents the querent, then the querent may not be ready to accept that information. However, it is your job to relay the message and allow the client to make her own choices with that information. Do not get emotionally connected to the outcome. You need to do only your best to give a good reading with kindness and compassion for your client.

STRENGTHENED BY: The Moon, Seven of Cups, Ten of Swords
WEAKENED BY: The Sun, the World, Ace of Wands
REVERSED MEANING: Coming clean, getting caught, lost object found

EIGHT OF SWORDS
Feeling trapped, self-limiting beliefs, restricted
MEANING: Ever have an issue that you felt you could think your way out of, but instead only made it worse by spiraling from one horrible hypothetical to another? That is the gist of the Eight of Swords. There is a feeling of being stuck and having no way out of a situation, but on closer reflection, it is possible to see a solution. The card depicts a person wearing a blindfold and who is loosely bound around the torso. The blindfold represents refusing to see an opportunity, perhaps because our own self-limiting beliefs keep us from seeing it. Eight swords stuck in the ground form a semicircle fortress around the person. At first glance, it seems as if this person

is completely trapped. However, if the person would shrug off the loose ties and remove the blindfold, it is obvious that there is no imprisonment at all, only the perception of it. Because this is the suit of Swords, much of this restricted feeling is mental. It is the problem we can create ourselves by overthinking and overanalyzing and telling ourselves there is no way out of this particular situation. Mind-set is reality. If you don't believe something can happen, it won't.

INTERPRETATION: When this card appears, the client may be in a bit of a mental pickle. She is probably feeling stuck, stagnant, or even trapped by a situation. The Eight of Swords requires a little detective work to get to the heart of what is causing this feeling. But I am hopeful when a client gets this card because it represents a problem that started through disordered thinking, one that can be fixed through small steps. Ultimately, the client can free herself. Suggest the sitter try affirmations. At times, we all fall prey to the negative inner voice or constant worrying. What we tell ourselves becomes our reality. So, if things have been overwhelming for a while and the sitter has only reinforced that situation by feeling as though she can never get out of it, simply stated, she won't. However, Spirit never wastes an opportunity to help turn a sitter's life around. Maybe she came for a general reading just to see what would come up and when this card appears, she ends up leaving, knowing that her life is about to change for the better. That is the amazing ability of any psychic reading.

STRENGTHENED BY: The Hanged Man, Two of Swords, Nine of Swords
WEAKENED BY: The Chariot, Ace of Wands, Knight of Wands
REVERSED MEANING: Freedom, bonds are broken, prisoner release

NINE OF SWORDS

Nightmares, stressed out, sleepless nights

MEANING: Okay, so the suit of Swords may not be the most fun journey of the tarot's Minor Arcana. However, it does serve a purpose  and helps us through those tough times in life. So, in that respect, it is a much-needed suit. In the Nine of Swords, someone sits up in bed, head in hands, while nine swords hang precariously overhead, representing mental strife. It seems as if this person has just awoken from a nightmare or hasn't slept at all due to stress. On the bottom of the bed is a carving of one person defeating another in a fight. The blanket features roses and all the different zodiac signs, representing that, no matter who we are, we are all susceptible to mental strain. The suit of Swords serves as a warning sign along the way. If you heed the warnings of the Two of Swords (page 100), you never end up at the Three of Swords (page 101). When you free yourself from your mental prison in the Eight of Swords (page 108), the Nine of Swords never materializes. But alas, we are only human, and our minds are dangerous playgrounds in which we sometimes find ourselves lost. And it is okay. That is what is so lovely about receiving a reading because finally the matter is addressed and an objective third party can help you see the path before you.

INTERPRETATION: When this card appears in a reading, I know my client needs a helping hand. She has taken the Eight of Swords' self-limiting beliefs and ratcheted them up into full-blown panic. Without a doubt I know this client is not sleeping well, if at all, and when she does, her sleep is probably teeming with nightmares. Life has reached a crescendo peak of stress for the sitter. It is important to realize that the sitter has reasons to be stressed out, and her feelings should not be invalidated by the reader. However, this card represents people who get too caught up in negative thinking and almost create the situations they fear the most. For example, the querent may be stressed over her job. She does not like it, but she needs money to pay bills. She is so consumed with worry about losing her job that she is sleeping less and showing up late, which ultimately results in her being let go. To her, it is her worst nightmare coming true. In reality, it is a self-fulfilling prophecy. When this card is drawn, ask the client to reach out to friends for help and to begin to combat that negative inner voice. I also advise that Spirit is showing this to let her know that she has the ability and strength to pull out of this mind-set.

STRENGTHENED BY: The Devil, the Tower, Eight of Swords
WEAKENED BY: The Hierophant, the Sun, Knight of Swords
REVERSED MEANING: Great sleep, peace of mind, depression lifts

TEN OF SWORDS

Over it, endings, breakdown

MEANING: I know the card looks bad. And the thing is, it is bad. But there is good news as well. Since this is the Ten of Swords, it signifies an end to a cycle, one in which there may have been much mental toil. So, while this card is not super positive, there is a silver lining. This card traditionally depicts a person lying on the ground with ten swords sticking into their back. Is the person dead? It looks that way at first glance, but there is still life left yet. The background shows a serene body of water with dark clouds dissipating. The Ten of Swords is a scene of the aftermath of a battle. The point

is this: What will be the person's next step? Does one stay pinned under the weight of a breakdown, or dust off the debris and head down a different path? It all hinges on the person's mind-set.

INTERPRETATION: When this card is pulled, the client is most likely at an all-time low. There is no nice way to say it. This can indicate the end of a relationship (romantic, friend, or business) or job. It can indicate an illness. The Ten of Swords is the breaking point everyone has. One too many things has occurred, and the querent probably feels about as bad as the person depicted on the tarot card itself. I never negate or invalidate how a client is feeling. My job is to offer an interpretation that will enable the client to help herself. No one wants to feel this way, but it is a part of life. There are lessons to be taken from it. Again, because this is the suit of Swords, the pain felt most will be within the mind. The good part is that, with a change of mind, the situation can be improved. Some degree of humility needs to be employed. A little self-reflection about what can be done differently in the future can help keep this situation from repeating. Although the sitter may feel that all is lost, while she still has breath, there are always more opportunities. Again, this is the end of a cycle, a painful, not-so-fun cycle, but, it's now over.

STRENGTHENED BY: Death, Ten of Wands, Nine of Swords
WEAKENED BY: Strength, the Sun, the World
REVERSED MEANING: Recovery, escaping disaster, feeling lighter

COURT CARDS
Gemini, Libra, Aquarius

Within the suit of Swords, the court cards represent the air signs of Gemini, Libra, and Aquarius. These charismatic individuals are thinkers with minds constantly in motion. They are problem solvers, think-tank members, and philosophers. If you're in the mood for a deep, late-night conversation that lasts until the sun comes up, you want an air sign. If you need someone to talk out a problem with, grab an air sign. These people have bubbly energy that is contagious, and they are charming and cunning all rolled into one. Sometimes, with such powerful minds, they can experience sleepless nights from worry or from falling down multiple internet rabbit holes. Once they've gotten a good night's sleep, however, they are right as rain and ready to talk your ear off once again!

PAGE OF SWORDS

Honest, excited, overthinker

MEANING: The Page of Swords is a youthful person (in age or spirit) who has all the mental jitteriness of someone excited for a new adventure. This page is depicted as a person standing on a rolling hill with sword pointed toward the sky while the breeze whips through the clouds and the page's hair. As with all pages, there is a lot happening internally, but it has not yet begun to take place externally. In this case, everything starts with a great idea. This person is normally the idea person in a friend group. Whether it's late-night thinking sessions or writing songs, poetry, or plays, the page loves mental gymnastics. The page's curiosity is contagious. This person knows how to get an idea across and can get others on board for their latest venture, whether it is a podcast, YouTube channel, or TikTok account. The suit of Swords is all about communication, and the page definitely has a way with words. Because there is so much mental activity within the Page of Swords, this person can also be prone to anxiety, nervous energy, and self-criticism. Sometimes, the page's heightened energy can be a lot for others if they are not prepared for so much verbal and mental stimuli. Three excellent examples of the Page of Swords are Aly Raisman (Gemini), Doja Cat (Libra), and Yara Shahidi (Aquarius). While they represent three different fields, each exhibits the airy excitement and honest takes of their respective signs.

INTERPRETATION: Seeing this card means the client is an exuberant, always-thinking person. This client will know every internet conspiracy theory and will be able to explain it all to her friends. She is a deep thinker, a layman's philosopher, and she will have many theories about the way the world works. Eager to get out there and try out her ideas, she does not shy away from trying new mental pursuits. Because the sitter may be much more cerebral than emotional, discussing her feelings may not be her strongest attribute. She may tend to bottle things up until she can no longer hold back and then she tends to have an emotional outburst. If this card represents a love interest for the querent, it is guaranteed that this person will bring much knowledge to the relationship—from quirky tips on how to boil an egg without water (it's possible) to ancient alien conspiracies. An element of excitement and engaging conversations will be central to this relationship. If the card relates more to the overall feel of a situation, the querent's interest has most likely been piqued, possibly teetering on obsessed, and there is much buzz about it.

REVERSED MEANING: Deceptive, withdrawn, lack of enthusiasm

KNIGHT OF SWORDS

Charging ahead, constant movement, on a mission

MEANING: All knights love to rush off in search of adventure, but the Knight of Swords tops them all. Charging full steam ahead without much thought about what-ifs, this knight is all about movement. This represents quickness of mind and body. Traditionally this knight is shown in a full suit of armor, sword raised confidently to the sky, on a white steed racing at breakneck speed. The armor has sharp edges, which represents the biting tongue and rapier wit of this knight. The clouds even seem to be moving quickly, all to illustrate the speed at which this knight accomplishes tasks. Tom Holland (Gemini), Noah Schnapp (Libra), and Harry Styles

(Aquarius) are excellent ambassadors for the cerebral, creative, and cunning Knight of Swords. Whether it is acting or singing, these individuals keep it witty and artistic, no matter what they do, and go all out, no brakes.

KNIGHT of SWORDS.

INTERPRETATION: When this card is pulled and represents the client, I know that she means business. All go and never settling for no, the client is probably filled with ideas and is on a mission to get them all done as quickly as possible. While the Page of Swords (page 113) was still ruminating on exciting ideas, the knight is now in full execution of them. The sitter may be someone who takes off on a project without too much thinking, which may get her into some trouble when consequences catch up. However, many people probably admire her for this attribute. If this card represents someone else in the querent's life, especially a romantic interest, the relationship is probably moving fast and full of late-night conversations and days of starting projects and creating. In the case of a work-related reading, this person may be too much to handle at times, as their approach may be short and to the point without much thought for feelings. It is not personal, as their mind is going all the time; however, it is not fun to be on the receiving end. When the Knight of Swords is pulled as the situation card, the sitter may be feeling as though things are moving too quickly or her energy is being pulled in a million different directions. At these times, it is a good idea to take a breath and step back from whatever is going on in order to assess it better. This can also represent a hint from Spirit that the client needs to step up and take a more aggressive and straightforward approach with a current issue.

REVERSED MEANING: Passive, fearful, taking the easy route

QUEEN OF SWORDS

Communicator, wise, sharp

MEANING: An excellent conversationalist with a sharp wit and keen insight, the Queen of Swords rules over all forms of communication. Always thinking, even when she should be sleeping, this queen knows when someone is lying without the person ever speaking a word. Although her demeanor can come off as cold and detached, there beats a heart of pure fire beneath the icy exterior. She sits on a throne carved with a cherub and butterfly. The cherub alludes to her soft underbelly while the butterfly relates to transformation. She has her left hand open to receive and holds her sword in her right. The queen in any suit has taken the exuberance and adventurous nature of the page and knight and melded them with hard-earned wisdom. This queen is no exception. She can be brutally honest and blunt with her words, but her mind is always moving much quicker than her mouth. Most times, the sting is unintentional—unless she means to throw daggers with her words, and then of course, watch out. Queens of biting insight and razor-sharp minds, Laverne Cox (Gemini), Serena Williams (Libra), and Shakira (Aquarius) all represent the Queen of Swords proudly. Each represents their field so superiorly that the thought of anyone else challenging their position on the throne seems ludicrous.

INTERPRETATION: When this card is pulled and represents the querent, without a doubt I know this is a person who does not suffer fools lightly. She is mentally agile and loves puzzles, mysteries, and maybe a bit of the latest gossip. While she is normally in control of her mental energy, sometimes it can become too taxing, even for her. For example, if the Queen of Swords card is flanked by the Nine of Swords (page 110) and Eight of Swords (page 108), the client is probably in need of a mental health break. Spirit is clever because it always seems to nudge a client to get a reading at just the right moment so it can give the sitter encouragement and help course correct. I would strongly advise that my client take some time off in order to have a mental reset. In a love reading where the Queen of Swords represents the love interest, it is easy to advise that the relationship will never be boring. In the case of this card representing a situation, the best course of action may be to communicate clearly and effectively and not be afraid to be honest.

REVERSED MEANING: Pessimistic, calculating, distrustful

KING OF SWORDS

High standards, shrewd, ambitious

MEANING: This king stares directly at you, unwavering and unyielding in his goals and aim in life. This person has a plan and sticks to it. His mind would be something amazing to break apart and study. Pictured on his throne with a piercing gaze, the king sits with his left arm relaxed and his right arm gripping his sword pointed toward the sky. Clouds float by in the background, representing the cerebral and changing nature of this individual. Excellent ambassadors of this kingly energy are Kendrick Lamar (Gemini), Donald Glover (Libra), and Christian Bale (Aquarius). Intense, creative, and undoubtedly talented, these three represent all that is amazing about the King of Swords.

KING of SWORDS.

INTERPRETATION: When this card is pulled and represents the client, I know that she is someone who is organized, has her stuff together, and holds herself, as well as those around her, to a high standard. Again, the king of any suit does not necessarily represent a male-gendered person. It simply represents these attributes. I also know that when this card is pulled that the sitter may have a hard time connecting emotionally. Intellectual pursuits are her personal playground, but feelings? Yuck! Surrounding cards may reveal what can help the client connect to her emotional side if that is what is being called for from Spirit. If this card is pulled in a love reading, the querent may be needing help on how to connect emotionally to this king in her life. While the King of Swords can be exciting to be with, as their mind is like a roller coaster, it can be difficult to keep up with that energy after a while. When this card represents a situation, it could be that the sitter needs to raise her standards and hold others accountable for the energy they are bringing to the table. This card can also represent a busy time in the sitter's life in which her ambitions can take her far.

REVERSED MEANING: Tyrant, vengeful, intolerant

✦ SUIT OF CUPS ✦
Water Energy / Summer / Months

Welcome to the suit of Cups! Ready to cry your eyes out and feel all the feels? Don't worry. It is not all ooey-gooey emotions. Cups also deal with the subconscious and your connection to the spiritual realm. The Cups are connected to the water signs of Cancer, Scorpio, and Pisces and are represented within the court cards. Water is known to be an amazing conduit between this world and the next, between the conscious and subconscious mind, and represents beautifully the liquid nature of emotions. This suit will delve into love and romance, the supernatural, the spiritual world, emotions, healing, and contentment. The Cups represent events that may take place in the summer. When calculating timing of an event, if the card pulled is a Cup, the time frame should occur within a matter of months.

ACE OF CUPS

Loving yourself, blessings overflow, spiritual awakening

MEANING: A hand appears through the clouds extending to you a chalice, overflowing with water, pouring down in five separate streams into a pool of water below, dotted with lotus flowers. The five streams represent the five senses while the water itself represents emotions and spiritual connections. The lotus blossoms are signs of a spiritual awakening. Above the cup is a dove diving down, representing the one source we are all connected to as well as your connection to your Higher Self. Aces are always new beginnings. Since the suit of Cups deals with emotions, romance, and the subconscious, this is a new beginning in terms of love, spiritual awakenings, and healing.

INTERPRETATION: This is a beautiful card to pull for a client. Many times, just by the first card selected, you can get a feel for how the entire reading will go. When the Ace of Cups appears first, I know the sitter is in store for some fresh energy, and the mood becomes hopeful and uplifting. Before we get into the romantic implications of this card, many times this card represents the sitter falling in love with herself. This is that lovely feeling, when you look into a mirror and think, "Darn, you're gorgeous." It does not happen all the time, but when it does, it is such an affirming experience. This is not narcissism, which is the opposite of positive self-esteem. This is about knowing your own worth and embracing your whole self. It is kind of a magical experience. I love to see it for my clients. This step needs to happen first so that, if a sitter is on the lookout for love, she will find it because she has first developed her own self-worth. How you love yourself teaches the Universe what type of partner to bring you. In terms of a romantic reading, this card usually means there is a new love on the horizon for the querent. She may not have met this person yet, but she is on the dating apps. She is open, and she is looking. This is also a great card to receive when there is a question about whether or not manifestations will come to fruition. This is a definite yes because literally your cup runneth over with blessings.

STRENGTHENED BY: The High Priestess, the Empress, the Star
WEAKENED BY: Death, Five of Cups, Eight of Cups
REVERSED MEANING: Unrequited love, self-loathing, spiritually lost

TWO OF CUPS
Budding romance, partnership, deep connection
MEANING: So, once you take care of knowing what you want and making sure you treat yourself as you want someone else to, the

Universe sends this lovely goody into your life. The timing is right for someone to show up that matches your energy. Traditionally, this card depicts two individuals facing each other, both holding a cup—the Two of Cups is *the* relationship card. Between the two individuals hovers a winged staff with two snakes intertwined around it, Caduceus of Hermes, which is a sign for exchange. Above that is a lion's head, which represents the fire sign of Leo and indicates there may be a lot of chemistry between these two people.

INTERPRETATION: This is one of the easiest answers to give when a client comes in for a love reading and pulls this card. The answer is, "Yes! This is the start of a beautiful romance!" If it is strengthened by surrounding cards, you may be looking at a soul mate connection, or at least a long-term relationship in the beginning stages. However, if it is weakened by surrounding cards, the reader may have to dampen the client's hopes and explain that things may not last too long in this budding romance. However, let's assume that everything looks positive, as it often does. This card has brand-new, first-date goodness, sweet first kisses, and all those butterflies-in-your-stomach vibes. Beyond romantic relationships, this card is also a positive sign for good working colleagues, business partnerships, and new friends coming into the querent's life. It also points to a peaceful and loving time in the querent's life in which all relationships are going well and are fulfilling at every level.

STRENGTHENED BY: The Lovers, Ten of Cups, Nine of Pentacles
WEAKENED BY: The Hermit, the Devil, Five of Cups
REVERSED MEANING: Separation, incompatibility, fight with a friend

THREE OF CUPS

Party time, guides, fun with friends

MEANING: Celebrate good times! Gather up your favorite people and let your hair down. This is a feel-good card with all your favor-

ite people. Three people cheer to each other, hoisting their cups into the air. The feeling is jubilant and celebratory. They are dancing, and cornucopias litter the ground, representing abundance and harvest. This depicts a group of friends that celebrate and lift each other up. There is an equality to the scene, as no one person is dominating the scene. Perhaps one person just got engaged while another got a promotion at work. Again, the Cups represent emotions, so these vibes are high, and the good feelings are flowing as much as the possible wine in their cups.

INTERPRETATION: This is another one of those cards that I love to see as a reader. It is about celebrating, having fun, letting loose, and feeling good around those who know you best. When this card is pulled, the client will be spending some quality time with those she loves. She may have received a raise at work, started a new job, recently moved into a new place, or embarked on any number of other life events that make you want to grab your best friends and celebrate. This card can also represent the sitter's getting in touch with her guides. Many times, I have pulled this card, and when I mention meditating or receiving signs from guides, my sitters usually exclaim that they have been having so many synchronistic experiences, such as seeing repeating angel numbers or finding pennies or feathers. I have also found this card represents ancestors reaching out and wanting to work with the querent.

STRENGTHENED BY: The Star, Three of Pentacles, Four of Wands
WEAKENED BY: The Hermit, the Hanged Man, Four of Cups
REVERSED MEANING: Gossip, excessive partying, friendship ends

FOUR OF CUPS

Contemplation, shut down, indifferent

MEANING: After the jovial energy of the Three of Cups (page 121), we experience a little bit of a lull with the Four of Cups. A person sits beneath a tree, arms crossed, and face contemplative. There are three cups in the foreground that the person does not seem to notice, as well as a fourth cup being extended from the ether itself. Again, the person seems more inwardly focused than observant of his surroundings. The cups represent opportunities the person could be receiving but is not acknowledging them at this time. It could be that the options are being weighed or that the person is too afraid to take a chance due to past experiences.

INTERPRETATION: When this card is pulled, the client may be taking a self-imposed sabbatical regarding new opportunities or has become so inwardly focused that she is missing out on seeing them. This is one of those instances where surrounding cards help to clarify the issue at hand. The sitter may be in a bad emotional space in which previous letdowns are inform-ing current decision-making. It can also rep-resent not seeing clear possibilities in front of you due to being focused on the wrong thing or not feeling as if the opportunities being pre-sented are "good enough." It is important to be sensitive to the client's feelings while still being honest and forthright about what the reading is saying. Sometimes, the querent needs to hear from a third party that there are new offerings

coming and to be on the lookout for them. Also, this can repre-sent the client taking a more meditative approach before choosing which option to take.

STRENGTHENED BY: The Hermit, Temperance, Two of Swords
WEAKENED BY: The Sun, Ace of Wands, Ace of Cups
REVERSED MEANING: Motivation, optimism, gratitude

FIVE OF CUPS

Grief, sorrow, angst

MEANING: The Five of Cups could be called the official bummer card of the tarot deck. Traditionally, it is illustrated with a figure draped in a black cloak, staring at three overturned cups that have spilled their contents. These represent something the person is disappointed or sad about. Behind the person, out of their view, stand two other cups. These represent possible opportunities that the person simply cannot see at this time. In the distance, there is a bridge crossing a river. At any time, the individual can head toward the horizon and get to the other side, where a castle beckons, but at the moment that does not seem to be the focus. The bridge stands for the ability to move beyond this current pain. It is up to the individual when that time will come. There is much emotional angst and sorrow depicted on this card. It cannot be inferred what situation causes the person's sadness, beyond the spilled cups, but it has consumed this individual's entire focus.

INTERPRETATION: Oh my goodness. When this card comes up in a reading, my heart immediately goes out to my client. Unless  the card is in the Future position, I know she is currently experiencing a difficult emotional time. This can appear right after a breakup, job loss, death of a loved one, illness, or any number of situations that can cause stress and sadness. While it normally does appear soon after one of these events, this card can also come up when the sitter has not let go of old wounds and hurts and is still affected by them. Based on surrounding cards, the client may need to be reminded that, while it is healthy to grieve, at some point it is best to move forward. The reader can point out that there are opportunities waiting for the sitter as soon as she turns her focus to the horizon. If the overall reading focuses on the sitter's emotional issue, this is another example of when it may be best to refer her to a licensed professional (page 24). Also, put yourself in your querent's shoes. Be mindful of the words you use when delivering a message. While it may be easy to say, "Move on. Get over it," how easy is it for you to do that in your own life and how would you want to receive this same advice from a reader? Being sensitive to your clients' needs will always help you get repeat business.

STRENGTHENED BY: The Tower, Three of Swords, Eight of Cups
WEAKENED BY: The Sun, Three of Cups, Ten of Cups
REVERSED MEANING: Acceptance, forgiveness, a warning against obsessing

SIX OF CUPS

Childhood, family life, innocence

MEANING: After the turmoil of the Five of Cups (page 123), the Six of Cups is a much-needed respite from heartache. This card focuses much more on the sweet memories of the past, particularly around one's youth. This card depicts a young boy who holds out a cup full of flowers to a younger girl. Another cup sits on a podium, also filled with flowers, while the remaining four sit in the foreground. An older person with a cane can be seen walking away in the background. The children are located center stage in an open plaza of a home. The image is sweet, innocent, and serene. As the children inhale the sweet aromas of the flowers, you, too, may find yourself thinking back on soft memories.

INTERPRETATION: Whenever this card pops up, I advise the client that someone from her childhood may be showing up unexpectedly. This could be a rekindling of a romance with a high school sweetheart or catching up with hometown friends. This card can also reflect a moment when a sitter may find herself flipping through old yearbooks or photo albums, thinking about the warm memories of her youth. This card can reflect dealing with some inner child healing, especially if it appears alongside the Star (page 63) or the Magician (page 31). Emotions may be running high as the sitter works through those feelings. Not everyone has a happy childhood, and it could be that the querent is having to relive some difficult situations. For the most part, this card is a positive omen, as it also points to innocence and childlike wonder at the wider world. The sitter may be experiencing awe at some new element of her life that she may have taken for granted before. This card can appear after a health scare, and there is a tendency to think about the past fondly and appreciate the ease with which life happened at that time.

STRENGTHENED BY: The Empress, the Star, Nine of Pentacles

WEAKENED BY: Eight of Swords, Nine of Swords, Eight of Cups

REVERSED MEANING: Looking ahead, breaking ties with the past, moving away from home

SEVEN OF CUPS

Escapism, noncommittal, delusion

MEANING: The warm and fuzzies from the Six of Cups (page 125) have now morphed into a bad acid trip, where trees have mouths

and up is down. Basically, there is some delusional thinking going on in this card. A person stands before a plethora of cups, seven in fact. Some contain wonderful things that represent home-, work-, and love-life fulfillment while others hold snakes, dragons, and a mystery under a shiny blanket. There are dark clouds swirling around the floating cups, representing some uncertainty. The person is also cast in shadows to reflect indecision. It is difficult to make a choice when all of the options are not so crystal clear. Unlike the Nine of Cups (page 128), this is not the wish card, but it can be thought of as the wishful thinking card. Just because you want something to happen does not mean it necessarily will, especially if it is working against you.

INTERPRETATION: This is a delicate card to navigate because, although you know there is some deluded thinking going on by the client, it is never a good idea to accuse someone. In addition, if the Seven of Cups appears with cards that strengthen its meaning of delusions, addictive tendencies, and lying to oneself, it is important to address this carefully with the sitter. It is important to deliver readings clearly and honestly, but always, always with kindness (page 24). The querent may be getting this reading desperately hoping for some help and clear guidance on what next step to take. So let your intuition guide you to be gentle with your message. This card is asking the querent to move out of the thinking and wishing phase and move into action mode. She should make sure to ground her thinking and assess the options a little more objectively, but then move forward and make a decision.

STRENGTHENED BY: The Devil, the Moon, Seven of Swords
WEAKENED BY: The Emperor, Ace of Wands, Knight of Swords
REVERSED MEANING: Clarity, shattered illusion, realistic

EIGHT OF CUPS

Walking away, endings, disappointment

MEANING: This is the "I'm out of here!" card. There is something lacking emotionally with the situation, and it is time to move on.

It is hard, but it is necessary. There is a person walking away from a stack of eight cups, arranged in such a way that suggests one is missing, representing the emotional loss felt by the individual. The moon casts a side-eye as the person walks away, almost as though saying, "Took you long enough." A body of water with craggy rock formations scatter the background, the water representing the emotional nature of this card and the mountainous terrain representing a difficult trek.

INTERPRETATION: If this card falls within the Present or recent Past positions, I know my client has taken a hard step to make a clean break over a situation. If it has fallen in the Future position, I know that she soon will. Either way, there is a lot of emotional turmoil because the sitter just made a major decision to step away from something that her heart had really wanted to work out. That is a big deal. It is hard. First of all, the client should be congratulated for taking that painful step. This can be in regards to a relationship, job, or passion project. The main theme is that it is something the querent was emotionally invested in. Something built up for a long time for the client to get to this point. It has been a long time coming.

STRENGTHENED BY: Wheel of Fortune, Death, the Hermit
WEAKENED BY: The Magician, the Lovers, Ace of Cups
REVERSED MEANING: Settling, staying put, hesitant

NINE OF CUPS

Happiness, emotional fulfillment, wishes come true
MEANING: Traditionally known as the wish card, the Nine of Cups is a very positive card. An individual sits on a wooden bench, arms

crossed, sly smile stretched across his face. There are nine golden cups arranged behind him on a deep blue draped table. These cups represent the emotional contentment felt when your dreams have come true. This card represents that feeling when all seems right with the world. The sun is shining. Your family is in a good place. Love is filling your heart. It is just a feel-good card.

INTERPRETATION: When this card is pulled and sits in the Outcome position, it is exciting to relay to the client. It means that what she has been wishing for will be coming true. If it is in the Present position, the client is already feeling the good vibes from this card. She is most likely feeling that everything is just right. For example, a wedding or an engagement may have just taken place. She may have just added to her family through a birth or adoption. The sitter should most definitely be feeling joyous. This card can indicate that it's a good time for the querent to celebrate the good things in life a little more. Abundance and love are overflowing. So, it is always nice to share that feeling with others. Big parties might be in order—or a great bucket-list family vacation. This is an excellent card to pull for manifesting. This is Spirit's go-to way of showing the querent that whatever she puts out into the Universe at this time will return in her favor. Go for it! This is also a great time to show gratitude for all of the blessings received.

STRENGTHENED BY: The Empress, Nine of Pentacles, Queen of Pentacles
WEAKENED BY: The Hermit, Three of Swords, Seven of Swords
REVERSED MEANING: Greed, restlessness, bitterness

TEN OF CUPS
Balanced home life, happily ever after, Divine love
MEANING: As this is the tenth card in this suit, it represents completion. In the case of the suit of Cups, it is the completion of an emotional journey. This is the penultimate card of feelings, and they are all good. This is pure bliss, overflowing good vibes, a rainbow moment incarnate. A couple, each with an arm wrapped around the other, extend their free arms to the sky. Their backs are turned to the viewer. They gaze at the rainbow overhead, which contains ten cups. Children dance and play at their feet. In the background stands a beautiful home with rolling green hills and a small stream.

INTERPRETATION: This is one of my favorite cards to pull for a client. There is no negative connotation associated with it at all. For example, if the client wants to know whether things will work out with her current partner, the answer is, "Yes, yes, a thousand times yes!" This is the happily-ever-after card. This points to a wonder-

ful family and home life, a tremendous love, and possibly a soul mate situation—all around, a blissful feeling of overflowing wealth of love and emotional harmony. Things should be going well for the sitter in regards to all family relationships, friendships, and partnerships. If that does not reflect her current situation, this card is a clear indication that it will reflect her future. This is a good omen to receive if the sitter is inquiring whether current family strife will be mended. This is also a positive card in terms of inquiring about fertility or adding to the family. This can even reflect a positive move in a job situation. If the querent is considering taking a new position or applying somewhere and this card is in the Outcome position, I would definitely advise her to make the move, as this will likely be a good financial and emotional move.

STRENGTHENED BY: The Sun, the World, Ten of Pentacles
WEAKENED BY: The Hermit, the Tower, Five of Cups
REVERSED MEANING: Dysfunctional family, dissatisfaction, emotional turmoil and chaos

COURT CARDS
Cancer, Scorpio, Pisces

Within the suit of Cups, the court cards represent the water signs of Cancer, Scorpio, and Pisces. These individuals are full of dark watery secrets and fluid emotions. They are caretakers, nurturers, and dreamers—and sometimes highly mysterious. If you need a shoulder to cry on, find a water sign. If you want someone to bake your favorite cookies and make chicken noodle soup when you're sick, get a water sign bestie. These people feel the full range of emotions that human beings experience and can channel them into beautiful art. They are singers, actors, and artists. Their hearts lead them through life. Being so in touch with all those feelings can get a bit overwhelming at times, but once they eat their favorite comfort food and have a good cry, you'll never find sweeter souls willing to help you no matter what.

PAGE OF CUPS

Dreamer, otherworldly, super creative

MEANING: Remember that the court cards are an embodiment of the ace through ten of each suit. So, the Page of Cups is the human

representation of the Ace of Cups (page 119). This person gets inspired by seemingly random and out-of-the-blue moments. In this deck, the page is dressed in a tunic covered in flowers with a decorative blue hat and matching oversized scarf. The blue represents water and its intuitive nature. It is said that more supernatural and paranormal events take place around water than dry land. Water is a conduit. In a way, so is the Page of Cups, who is able to channel the creative energies that came out of nowhere and turn them into great creative endeavors. The page holds one cup with a fish popping out of it. This represents that surprising element of inspiration. You never know when it might strike. Chloe Bailey (Cancer), Willow Smith (Scorpio), and Millie Bobby Brown (Pisces) are perfect embodiments of the Page of Cups. They all share a sense of wonder, chase their dreams with no other intention other than to chase it, and know that if they can dream it, they can achieve it.

INTERPRETATION: When this card is pulled and it represents the client, I envy her a little bit. As a Virgo, I normally have to plan before even starting to plan. However, the Page of Cups personality follows the flow of the beat of her heart. You know in cartoons when a character smells something divine and they float along the air to find it? That is the Page of Cups. She lets her inspiration carry her through life. This card can represent the client being struck with some inspiration and wanting to chase it. It is also an excellent omen for receiving psychic insights and intuitive hits. The querent should be open to tapping into that facet of herself and seeing where it leads. If this represents the situation itself, it may be that the sitter needs to inject a little of the Page of Cups' take on life. Look for ways to be inspired and make choices based on what feels good intuitively.

REVERSED MEANING: Directionless, unused creative talents, jealousy

KNIGHT OF CUPS
Artistic, romantic, emotionally available
MEANING: This is the knight all the other knights are supposed to be in the fairy tales. The one who will rescue you while also

respecting your autonomy, rub your feet and make you cocoa, and kill bugs and slay dragons. This individual makes the ideal romantic partner. Pretty simple and straightforward, the depiction on the card is that of a knight upon a pony with a cup extended. The cup represents an offer of love, or at least emotional closeness. A river runs along the background, cutting through a desert landscape. Maybe things have been a bit dry in the love department, but when this knight arrives, heavenly rains may fall. Post Malone (Cancer), Taron Egerton (Scorpio), and Bad Bunny (Pisces) make amazing candidates as the Knight of Cups. Funny, sexy, and creative, these three set hearts aflame through their emotional availability as the characters they play or through the songs they sing.

INTERPRETATION: When this card represents the client, I know she is a hopeless romantic. She believes in happily ever after and is waiting for hers to arrive. She has a giving heart and loving energy. If this represents a possible love interest for the sitter, she can rest assured that she will be emotionally fulfilled by this relationship. This person will most likely be the sort to bring flowers and candies, remember her favorite songs, and make instant friends with her pets. When this card represents the situation, a loving heart is needed to help sort through the issue. It would best if good intentions lead the way and help the querent figure out what to do. This card can also appear when the sitter is entering a prolific emotionally expansive and creative period in her life. She may finally be ready to pursue artistic endeavors, such as painting, interior decoration, or interpretive dance—or begin to teach others how to tap into their heart space to create more love in the world.

REVERSED MEANING: Heartache, moodiness, closed off emotionally

QUEEN OF CUPS

Nurturing, giver, highly intuitive

MEANING: This is the mother of all mothers card. Highly intuitive, sensitive, giving, and nurturing, the Queen of Cups is in touch with the mystical and mundane. Pictured sitting on her throne carved with sea creatures, this queen holds an ornate cup. It has winged handles and jewels, and it is covered, unlike other cups in the suit. This shows her wisdom comes from the unseen. Her throne is positioned at the edge of

a body of water, and her feet rest on pebbles. This represents that she is in touch with her emotions but not overwhelmed by them. Her robe is blue and reflects the water all around her. Missy Elliot (Cancer), Gabrielle Union (Scorpio), and Rihanna (Pisces) are prime examples of the Queen of Cups vibe. They are able to convey universally felt emotions through their music and acting and also seem to have a direct connection to the zeitgeist, as they tend to be trendsetters in their respective fields. These are the types that feel their way into whatever they pursue.

INTERPRETATION: When this card is pulled and represents the client, she is the epitome of a caring and nurturing individual. She follows her intuition, and it rarely steers her wrong. Based on surrounding cards, it could be that she currently feels emotionally overwhelmed and needs to lean a little more on her head than her heart at this time. When this card represents someone in the querent's life, especially a love interest, the relationship will be overflowing with love and care. This person will make breakfast in bed, snuggle at all times, and watch any romance movie the querent wants. This person may be a little clingy at times as well and, without someone to care for, can become a little lost. When this card represents a situation, it's best approached with an open heart. Maybe a little TLC is all that is needed to correct the issue. This card can also represent someone getting pregnant or adding to a family. In addition, the Queen of Cups is more powerful in terms of receiving psychic insights or intuitive guidance than the Page (page 131) or Knight of Cups (page 132). That youthful excitement of finding out what you suspected was true is met with a worldly wisdom gained through experience, and this allows a person to be able to guide herself through her inner knowing.

REVERSED MEANING: Smothering, heavy-handed, selfish

KING OF CUPS

Diplomatic, emotionally balanced, counselor

MEANING: Matching the Ten of Cups (page 129) energy of completion and emotional harmony, the King of Cups is the human equivalent of a wise and emotionally balanced ruler.

KING of CUPS.

He has mastered the flutters and flits of his heart and incorporates it into decision-making: his emotions are weighed equally, but not more so, than his intellect. If the Queen of Cups is the ultimate mother, the King of Cups is the ultimate father, at least the more balanced version than the Emperor (page 37) represents. The King of Cups is our current concept of a good father—in touch with his emotions, not afraid of yours—while still offering guidance to keep you on the right path. That's not too much to ask, right? On the card, this king sits upon his throne, floating on a slab in the middle of a fluid body of water. This shows his mastery over his emotions. Not that he does not use them, just that they do not overtake him. He is the Knight of Cups (page 132) all grown up. Benedict Cumberbatch (Cancer), Ryan Reynolds (Scorpio), and Antoni Porowski (Pisces) know how to be in their feels and yet not overdone by them. Each is known for his ability to tap into the emotional spectrum and make you feel something deeply, whether it be through acting, comedy, or even a well-cooked meal.

INTERPRETATION: When this card is pulled and represents the client, it is obvious this person is emotionally balanced and has integrated youthful free-loving energy with the wisdom of knowing how to keep emotions in check, keeping her life on an even keel. This person knows when to pull out all the stops to open her heart space, but also knows when not to. Whereas the Page or Knight of Cups may get overly emotional about situations and lose sight of their goals, the King of Cups is cool as a cucumber without moving into the icy dominion of the King of Swords (page 117). When this card represents a love interest for the client, this relationship will likely be emotionally fulfilling and an equal partnership. If the sitter's love language is physical touch and words of affirmation, this individual will probably make a good match. If there are some warning sign cards accompanying it, such as the Devil (page 59) or the Three of Swords (page 101), this person may have taken the control of their emotions to the extreme and somehow stumbled into being more emotionally unavailable than the querent would like. When this card represents a situation at hand, the advice is to move forward with the knowledge that how the querent's heart feels about it is probably the best summation of the events. Trust in your feelings but keep a balanced approach.

REVERSED MEANING: Insensitive, trouble expressing emotions, holding a grudge

✦ SUIT OF PENTACLES ✦
Earth Energy / Fall / Years

Finally! It's the Suit of Pentacles! This suit is the eldest of the four suit siblings. Pentacles have seen it first and made all the mistakes first. So, they are more than capable of passing down their wisdom to their younger siblings, the Cups, Swords, and Wands. The Pentacles represent the earth zodiac signs of Taurus, Virgo, and Capricorn in the form of the court cards. In the ace through ten, they deal with the physical elements of life, such as work, money, health, and home life. The Pentacles represent the fall season. When calculating the timing of an event, if the card pulled is a Pentacle, the time frame should occur within a matter of years. Remember, this suit takes its time, but does it right. Quality takes time. Let's roll up our sleeves and see what the Pentacles can teach us.

ACE OF PENTACLES

New money opportunity, investment, fresh start

MEANING: Aces are those golden opportunities that start you on an entirely new path. The Ace of Pentacles deals with financial growth as long as the time and determination are put into it. This is not a get-rich-quick scheme. This is something that, when nurtured, will turn into tremendous abundance. Similarly depicted as the other aces, the Ace of Pentacles shows an extended, floating hand, offering a large pentacle within it. In the background is a lush garden scene with a few mountain peaks behind. This indicates the growth possibility, but not without work and dedication.

INTERPRETATION: This is an exciting card to pull for any client. It signifies a new opportunity and one in an area that most people worry about—finances. This can come in the form of a job opportunity, but it may not be that dream job. It could be the get-a-foot-in-the-door job that then leads to the dream job. Think of this card as a seed. It needs time, water, sunlight, and soil in order to reach its full potential. A seed may not look like much upon first inspection, but over time a seed can turn into a multitude of things. A tall oak comes from a seed. A bountiful harvest first starts as tiny seeds. So, I advise clients to not look at this opportunity and dismiss it due to its lack of flash. This card can also represent a small amount of money that can then be turned into more through investments. It can also be a small step the sitter takes that will have big implications later in her life, such as taking a class, picking up a new hobby, or exploring a natural talent. Remember, the Pentacles' timing happens in increments of years. So, nothing is going to happen overnight with this suit, but what does transpire will be well worth the wait.

STRENGTHENED BY: The Empress, Ace of Wands, Seven of Pentacles
WEAKENED BY: Eight of Swords, Eight of Cups, Knight of Swords
REVERSED MEANING: Unexpected expense, financial hardship, overspending

TWO OF PENTACLES

Juggling responsibilities, multitasker, busy time

MEANING: So, you took the first steps in the Ace of Pentacles (page 137) and now things are rocking and rolling, maybe a little

bit more than anticipated. It is all there in the card. A person stands apparently juggling two pentacles linked together by the sign of infinity. In the background is a rolling sea with two boats, one going up while the other is going down. This represents the highs and lows of life and suggests that, while there is much going on, it is important to find the balance. The infinity sign points to a limitless ability to earn as long as there is proper focus and dedication to the tasks at hand. This is the card of the multitasker. There are many responsibilities to be juggled, but they are manageable.

INTERPRETATION: When this card pops up in a reading, the client most likely has her hands full with many responsibilities; it is a busy time of life. This card can show up when someone is in the thick of parenthood: playing carpool parent, hustling from one sport to a dance recital, and basically trying not to scream into the abyss at any point in the day. This can also represent a busy time in regards to work or business. The sitter may have taken a leap with that Ace of Pentacles moment and now things are taking off. It is a good problem to have but still comes with its own inherent stressors. Based on surrounding cards, such as the Nine of Swords (page 110), this card can also be a reminder for the querent to try to find some balance in her life. Maybe she is trying to juggle one too many things. It is a good idea to prioritize and perhaps shed one or two tasks in order to keep moving forward without hitting the proverbial wall.

STRENGTHENED BY: Justice, Temperance, Three of Wands
WEAKENED BY: Seven of Cups, Nine of Swords, Ten of Wands
REVERSED MEANING: Dropping the ball, overwhelmed, imbalance

THREE OF PENTACLES

Teamwork, help is coming, collaborative project

MEANING: Now it's a party! We are moving right along on this suit of Pentacles journey. A seedling has been planted, sprouts have shot up, and now comes the time when it is apparent a couple of helping hands would certainly come in, well, handy. In this card the Three of Pentacles depicts three individuals discussing some plans for a cathedral. Two seem to be architects, holding plans, while the third is the stonemason, most likely making another change for the umpteenth time based on their recommendations. The pentacles are carved within the arch and represent the skill

of the craftsmen involved. A church cannot be built by one person alone, and neither can a dream.

INTERPRETATION: When this card appears, help is on the way for the querent's goals. Most likely, she has gotten underway on her plans but may be finding she needs a little extra support. Spirit likes to use this card to reassure the sitter that her guides are showing up for her on the Other Side, and on this side, there will be resources available, too. This can also represent bringing on partners or investors to help build the client's business. The card can serve as a good job from Spirit, signifying that progress is being made. The client may be surprised by how much backing she receives from her friends and family, and this is a reminder to keep up the good work. This card can also pop up when an invitation to become part of a team occurs. The client may receive a promotion or take on a side project that will have her working with others, taking her to the next level in her career.

STRENGTHENED BY: The Star, Three of Cups, Seven of Pentacles
WEAKENED BY: The Hermit, the Hanged Man, Two of Swords
REVERSED MEANING: Refusing help, job loss, feeling rejected

FOUR OF PENTACLES
Hoarding, lack mind-set, fear of loss
MEANING: Come on, let go. Let me have it. It's okay. You have plenty. You do not have to hoard. See, this can happen sometimes

once you chase your Ace of Pentacles (page 137) moment, get started, receive help, and then start reaping some of those early returns. You get scared that's all there is, and you try to hold on to it. The good news is there is more where that came from. No need to hang on so tightly. Besides, it is hard to receive more when your hands are closed around what you already have. This card depicts a person sitting with both feet covering two pentacles, one pentacle balanced on top of their head, and the last one being bear-hugged to death. This represents a fear of loss. When it has taken time for abundance to build up, it is a natural reflex to try to hold on to that—but this is taking it too far. It has become a problem, as the worry has gripped the person and they are now stuck in place. There is so much more to look forward to. This journey needs to get back on track.

INTERPRETATION: When this card comes up in a reading, the client may be experiencing a lack mind-set. There could have been a recent large expense or an unexpected bill that came up that, although manageable, made the client feel a little money insecure. In its most positive light, it shows that the sitter has accumulated enough to worry about losing it, but she may have let herself get mired in it. The best advice to offer here is to remind the querent that she has made great strides, and in order to continue building that growth, she needs to ease up on the penny-pinching. As counterintuitive as it may seem, the more you let money flow, both in and out, the easier it returns back to you.

STRENGTHENED BY: The Devil, Four of Cups, Five of Pentacles
WEAKENED BY: Ace of Cups, Nine of Pentacles, Ten of Cups
REVERSED MEANING: Generosity, letting go, need to save

FIVE OF PENTACLES

Depletion, financial loss, refusing help

MEANING: We have now moved into a real loss—not just the worry of it from the Four of Pentacles (page 140). This isn't a self-fulfilling prophecy, but it can happen when we get fixated on loss rather than growth. Traditionally, this card depicts two individuals, one on crutches and the other covered in tattered clothes, walking barefoot in the snow right outside a stainglassed window containing all five pentacles. This represents individuals down on their luck

in real need and pain, but they are so focused on their troubles that they may be missing the help right in front of them. The five pentacles in the window may be a clue that the building contains the solace they so desperately seek.

INTERPRETATION: First of all, be mindful of the client's situation when this card is pulled. She may be dealing with financial difficulties, sickness, a job loss, or a one-sided relationship. Overall, this card deals with depletion. So, the client can be feeling depleted in many areas of life. If this card appears with cards that weaken it, which means they lessen the impact on the sitter, the message to deliver is that this time is passing. However, if other cards surround it that strengthen it, then this situation may be lasting longer. The main point of this card is to make the querent aware that there is no need to try to take on all these problems alone. In fact, there is help out there, but she may be too zoned in on her troubles to realize it. Ask questions that will lead the querent to think about her resources. Does she have any friends or family she could turn to? Is there a religious or spiritual outlet? Are there governmental programs she hasn't considered? There is a silver lining here, but she must lift her head to see it in the clouds overhead.

STRENGTHENED BY: Four of Pentacles, Five of Wands, Five of Swords
WEAKENED BY: The High Priestess, the Sun, Three of Pentacles
REVERSED MEANING: Improved finances, debts paid, help is denied

SIX OF PENTACLES
Generosity, charity, reciprocity
MEANING: Yay! Say goodbye to the loss of the Five of Pentacles (page 141) and say hello to the reciprocal nature of giving and receiving of the Six of Pentacles. In this scene, a person is handing out coins to beggars with one hand while holding a scale with the other, representing fairness and balance. The six pentacles take up the free space around the person's head and torso. This card can work on two levels. Sometimes, you are the generous giver, passing on your wealth to those in need. And sometimes, you are the needy recipient, gratefully receiving what others are generously offering.

INTERPRETATION: The surrounding cards provide the context of which role the client will be taking when it is drawn. If it is surrounded by those that strengthen it, then the client will most likely be in the giver's seat. Isn't this how it normally happens anyway? Have you ever struggled with money? If so, it is not something easily forgotten. Once you have gained a foothold in finances, when someone else is in need, you're usually more than willing to give what you can to help. If the card is surrounded by those cards that weaken it, the querent may be receiving rather than giving, which is still  a positive. What is more heartwarming than receiving help from those who love you at just the right moment? Either way you look at this card, it is definitely a positive and one of those singular cards that points to the beauty of the human spirit and our willingness to pull together when needed.

STRENGTHENED BY: The Chariot, Justice, Three of Pentacles
WEAKENED BY: Seven of Cups, Seven of Wands, Four of Pentacles
REVERSED MEANING: Scams, stinginess, greed

SEVEN OF PENTACLES

Putting in the work, long-term goals, accumulating

MEANING: The sevens of any suit have a wonky sort of energy to them. You're not quite at your goal yet, but too far down the road to turn back now. In the case of the Seven of Pentacles, hard work is being put in. The card depicts a scene with a person leaning on a shovel, gazing at a large bush full of seven pentacles. The individual seems to be reflecting and possibly taking a slight break after producing so much. Although it seems like this harvest is ready, there is still some time yet before that happens. This card shows that in-between time when you must continue going because you're almost at the finish line but you are tired from how much work you have already put in.

INTERPRETATION: When this card comes up in a reading, the sitter may be feeling restless. She may be asking, "Where is my abun-

dance? Where is the payoff for everything I've worked for?" It is a valid question when someone has reached a certain point in life. There has been a lot of hard work accomplished, and it is only natural to want to see some of the dividends. The best advice to give, although not the most exciting to hear, is to hold on a bit longer because she is almost there. This is a good moment to take stock of how far one has come. Celebrate every milestone. Take pride in what has been accomplished so far. This is a good time to take a small break or rest. Maybe a vacation is needed if work has been hard. Once you're rejuvenated, get back at it because the goal is almost at hand.

STRENGTHENED BY: The Emperor, Nine of Wands, Two of Pentacles
WEAKENED BY: The Fool, the Hanged Man, Four of Pentacles
REVERSED MEANING: Procrastination, listless, throwing in the towel

EIGHT OF PENTACLES

Mastery, craftsman, expertise
MEANING: After the slump of the Seven of Pentacles (page 143), the Eight of Pentacles finds you hitting your stride. This is when you're in a groove and work flows easily. The card depicts a person chiseling a pentacle into a disc while completed pentacles are displayed. This is the card of the craftsman, an expert in their field. The town is far in the background, representing that this person has made

work a priority and is enjoying the process. With each new pentacle produced, the person is mastering the skill.

INTERPRETATION: When this card appears, there is a level of mastery the client is attaining. If the card is in the Present position, this is something the client has already started, such as taking college courses, community classes, or online training. It could also be further education or training at work to help her reach the next level in her career. This card also pops up when a sitter is about to be recognized for her expertise in a field. She may be called in to work on a special project or decide to start a podcast or other outlet to pass on her knowledge to others. This is a busy time in the querent's life, but one in which she feels fulfilled and enjoys improving each and every day. Because this is under the suit of Pentacles, this mastery will pay off for the querent in terms of money and a job well done. If the sitter does not confirm that she is working on mastering a skill or taking up new training, this could be a gentle nudge from Spirit to start thinking about doing just that.

STRENGTHENED BY: The Emperor, Judgement, Nine of Pentacles
WEAKENED BY: The Devil, Nine of Swords, Seven of Cups
REVERSED MEANING: Poor quality, ready to quit, giving up too soon

NINE OF PENTACLES

Coming into your own, comfort, enjoyment

MEANING: Finally! That sweet spot of being recognized for the hard work you've put in and reaping the rewards of success has arrived! The card says it all on this one. A nicely dressed individual stands directly in the center of a bountiful scene. There are bunches of succulent grapes ripe for the picking all around. Nestled within those vines are the nine pentacles. A falcon sits perched on the person's hand, a sign of wealth and status as well as a degree of control. It has taken determination and effort to get to this point in life. The entire scene is lush and represents all that has been worked on and cared for is now coming to fruition.

INTERPRETATION: I love seeing this card come up for a client! What's not to be excited about? If it is in the Present position, the client is already well aware of her good fortune, but when this card appears

in the Future position, it is so satisfying to relay the message that good times are on the way. It is a time to splurge and be pampered. What is the point of all that hard work and time spent dedicated to something if there is no reward at the end of it? It is easy to get stuck in the go, go, go energy of staying busy with work, but this card is a reminder to stop and enjoy the fruits of your labor. This card can appear when the client is about to level up, financially speaking. I have seen this card appear when a sitter pays off a big car loan or even a mortgage. This represents being content and happy with home life. This is also a time of really coming into your own. You know your worth and you are not afraid to ask for it. Being comfortable in your own skin is reflected in this card as well. It is one of the most positive cards in the tarot.

STRENGTHENED BY: The Sun, the World, Nine of Cups

WEAKENED BY: Wheel of Fortune, Four of Pentacles, Five of Wands

REVERSED MEANING: Self-doubt, ungrateful, feeling empty

TEN OF PENTACLES

Success, contentment, abundance

MEANING: The ultimate culmination card, the Ten of Pentacles brings success, contentment, and abundance. It is the job well done card. The scene shown on the card centers on an older individual, who it is assumed by this point in life has accumulated great wealth. There are two dogs waiting for their master's commands or attention. There is also a younger couple with a small child, all within an opulent home. This is where all the pieces have come together. The entire view encompasses a life well spent and rewards hard earned. The white hair of the person indicates not only advanced age but also wisdom, which has brought abundance for oneself and the next generation.

INTERPRETATION: This is not a card that comes up in every reading, but when it does, it is certainly to be celebrated. This reflects that the client has come a long way and is in a state of having everything she desires. There is no wanting here. Home life, work, health, and love are all doing well. If the client wants to know whether or not something she is about to start will end well and this card shows up in the Outcome position, I would bet money on that venture being highly successful. I, in fact, may ask whether I can get in on the ground floor of whatever she is about to start (kidding, sort of). This is obviously a positive card. The only downside may be that it is a sign of completion and coming to the end of a journey. But if someone has garnered these kinds of results before, she certainly can, and most likely will, again.

STRENGTHENED BY: The Sun, the World, Ten of Cups
WEAKENED BY: Three of Swords, Seven of Cups, Five of Pentacles
REVERSED MEANING: Financial loss, lack, broken family

COURT CARDS

Taurus, Virgo, Capricorn

Within the suit of Pentacles, the court cards represent the earth signs of Taurus, Virgo, and Capricorn. These individuals get their hands dirty to make their hearts full. They are organizers, CEOs, volunteers, and pesky perfectionists. If you're having a party, the earth signs planned it and saw to every detail, making for a phenomenal night of fun. If you want accurate taxes and an excellent financial planner, again, seek out an earth sign. These people are the big brothers and sisters of the tarot court cards. They have lived some life, learned the lessons, and are more than willing to pass on their wisdom—sometimes, a little too willing. Due to their inner drive and connection to Mother Earth, these individuals can get pulled too thin from juggling so many responsibilities. But once they recenter and ground themselves, you will never find a more stable friend or ally on this planet.

PAGE OF PENTACLES

Student, eager learner, new interest

MEANING: Much like the Ace of Pentacles (page 137), this human equivalent is excited about learning something new, and since it is in the suit of Pentacles, it is something to do with the material world. A young person stands in a beautiful field admiring a large pentacle. Both feet are still planted on the ground, so no movement has begun toward goals. The background is fertile with possibilities, but the mountains show there may be some obstacles to overcome in order to meet these newfound goals. JoJo Siwa (Taurus), Zendaya (Virgo), and Gabby Douglas (Capricorn) are mighty representatives of the Page of Pentacles energy. They are enthusiastic, ready to learn something new, and already masters of their fields.

INTERPRETATION: When this card appears, the client is getting ready to start on a new journey, one dealing with the material realm. So, this may take the form of starting college, taking a class, picking up a new hobby, or deciding to finally chase a lifelong dream. The energy is youthful, but the client does not necessarily have to be. In universities all over the world, there have been graduates well into their seventies, eighties, and even nineties. An interest in learning can be a lifelong pursuit. This card also pops up in a reading when the sitter is about to start a new job or maybe take on new responsibilities in a current role. This is an exciting moment for the sitter.

She is most likely experiencing heightened emotions around the thought of getting started on this new passion project. Her energy levels are probably going to be high, and her enthusiasm is likely to be contagious.

REVERSED MEANING: Apathy, lack of common sense, unorganized

KNIGHT OF PENTACLES
Methodical, disciplined, slow and steady

MEANING: The knight is starting to take the steps the page was dreaming of. While all of the knights are ready to head off toward the horizon, this is the most disciplined and most thoughtful knight of the tarot deck. This knight sits upon a black steed holding a pentacle aloft. The background shows a field with neatly plowed rows. This represents the knight's meticulous nature. Joe Kerry (Taurus), Gaten Matarazzo (Virgo), and Timothée Chalamet (Capricorn) make fabulous fill-ins for the Knight of Pentacles. These individuals are nerdy chic, controlled, and know that slow and steady win the race.

INTERPRETATION: This card is a great indicator that the client is ready to put in the work to achieve her goals. This might not be the

flashiest or most creative pursuit, but it is one that pays off in the end. When this card is pulled, the sitter is most likely embarking on a goal that will take time and dedication to achieve. If this appears along with the Sun (page 67) or the World (page 71), the outcome will be sensational. If this card represents someone else in the querent's life, especially a romantic interest, this person will be faithful, steadfast, and true. While things may come off a little boring for some,

with the right partner this person can make an attentive and caring lover. If this card represents the situation at hand for the client, a methodical and well-planned approach should be taken. There may be much chaos or impatience happening within or around the sitter, and so it would be prudent to take a more controlled view of the situation. The Knight of Pentacles can also represent a rather mundane cycle of life. Things may be feeling a little rote and routine. Perhaps the sitter is looking for a little spice and variety. If this card appears with the Wheel of Fortune (page 49) or Chariot (page 43), there is a good chance things are about to turn a corner and the sitter will see the momentum shift.

REVERSED MEANING: Irresponsible, anxious, careless

QUEEN OF PENTACLES

Earth mother, service oriented, trailblazer

MEANING: All hail the queen! These are the rocks, the oaks, and the mountains of the tarot deck. This queen has a deep connection with nature because of the Pentacles' connection to the material world. This is a down-to-earth person, who can have a larger-than-life personality but stay rooted and keep her head about her. Depicted on her throne, this queen cradles her pentacle in her lap, representing her natural instinct for nurturing. All around her are symbols of life and growth and abundance in the physical world.

There are animals at her feet, flowering blossoms around the entire scene, and green fertile hills in the background. This all shows her deep affiliation with the world around her. It feeds her, and she in turns gives back to it. Three queens in every sense of the Pentacles word are Lizzo (Taurus), Beyoncé (Virgo), and Dolly Parton (Capricorn). These game-changing, fierce-yet-firm individuals have kept their feet on the ground while their heads have been  filled with dreams that they accomplish—all while looking amazing and still feeling approachable and relatable. How do they do it? It is the magic of the suit of Pentacles.

INTERPRETATION: When this card is pulled and represents the client, she most likely puts others before herself. In the queen form, unlike with the Page (page 148) or Knight of Pentacles (page 149), the client should have a balanced approach to doing for others while also maintaining healthy boundaries and providing self-care. The Queen of Pentacles represents the sitter being a generous and nurturing person. She is probably great with animals and babies, an amazing cook, and an excellent teacher. There is not much this queen cannot do. The bonus part is she normally stays humble about it all. When this card represents someone else in the querent's life, especially a love interest, there will be much care and deep connection within the relationship. This person will probably take care of the sitter's every need before she even realizes she needs it. If the card represents a situation at hand, the best approach would be to suggest a calm and rational approach with a tenderness of touch.

REVERSED MEANING: Materialistic, manipulative, insecure

KING OF PENTACLES

Grounded, wealthy, sensible

MEANING: This is the last king of the tarot, and it certainly shows. This king carries the wisdom, the patience, and the aptitude of a person who has gained all the lessons the Page (page 148) and Knight of Pentacles (page 149) have yet to attain. Through that knowledge and practical experience, this king has the Midas touch. He is surrounded by wealth and abundance. He likes to take care of those around him. If he's eating well, his family and friends are, too. Represented traditionally as a regal ruler sitting on a throne carved with bulls to represent his connection to the zodiac sign of Taurus, he holds a scepter in his right hand and the pentacle in his left. His robe is covered in grapes and their accompanying vines to signify his connection to the physical world and the abundance he can produce within it. No better representatives can be found for the King of Pentacles than Dwayne "The Rock" Johnson (Taurus), Idris Elba (Virgo), and Denzel Washington (Capricorn). These three certainly channel the King of Pentacles energy with their mental and physical know-how along with their desire to lift up those around them.

INTERPRETATION: When this card represents the sitter, she is a grounded individual who not only knows how to rise to the top but also cares enough to bring others with her. "A rising tide floats all boats" is certainly a phrase that would apply to this kind of person. This may be a contented and satisfying time in the sitter's life, as this type of individual enjoys the fruits of her labor. If this card represents a romantic interest for the client, then money and stability should be no problem in the relationship. This person will not force their significant other to take their path, but they are there for support whenever their partner may want it. If there is a

KING of PENTACLES.

situation at hand and this card is pulled to reflect it, a steady and measured approach would probably be what works best to sort it out. This can also represent a person in the sitter's life who will open doors for her and help set her up for success.

REVERSED MEANING: Corrupt, out of control, business failure

CONCLUSION

You see you had nothing to worry about, right? Tarot may seem intimidating at first, but once you get to know the cards, you can help yourself and your friends out of life's many jams in no time. You can start each morning with a card to get a sneak peek at the day ahead or develop a spread that can help you see into the next year. Tarot is super portable, and you can throw a few cards almost anywhere you go to get some guidance. This can become a part of your personal spiritual practice or even turn into a new career path. A positive side effect of consistent practice is a strengthened intuition. If you decide to take your skills to the next level, remember that an energy exchange takes place between you and your sitter. Requiring payment is not only okay—it helps to keep the energy exchange balanced. However you choose to incorporate tarot into your life, all the elements needed are present. If I have done my job correctly, and I certainly hope I have, you no longer need my helping hand. I leave you now with this simple wish:

May your days be filled with more joy than sadness.
May your heart be filled with more love than madness.
May you take this sacred tool and know that the more you use it,
the more you'll grow.

ACKNOWLEDGMENTS

Thank you to my dear editor, John Foster, who helped guide this series into all it could be. I am forever in his debt for making a dream of mine come true. I would also like to acknowledge the tremendous love and support my husband and children have given me. They are my biggest cheerleaders and greatest inspirations. I must also give a huge thank you to my online community at Namaste Magical. My work wouldn't be possible without you. Last, but certainly not least, I have to express my gratitude to Spirit, who I know conspired from beyond the veil to bring all of this to fruition. Thank you from the bottom of my heart. I hope this work makes you proud.

ABOUT THE AUTHOR

 April Wall is an international psychic medium with twenty years of experience helping clients sort through life's ups and downs. A proud Romany, she carries on the traditions started by the strong women in her family, especially her great-grandmother, great aunt, and granny, or as she refers to them, April's Angels. She lives with her husband, two kids, two doggies, and one spoiled kitty. Find her online at namastemagical.com to book a reading, and keep up to date through her social media accounts by following her on Instagram and TikTok @namastemagical.

weldon**owen**

an imprint of Insight Editions
P.O. Box 3088
San Rafael, CA 94912
www.weldonowen.com

CEO Raoul Goff
VP Publisher Roger Shaw
Editorial Director Katie Killebrew
Senior Editor John Foster
Editorial Assistant Kayla Belser
VP Creative Chrissy Kwasnik
Art Director Allister Fein
Designer Debbie Berne
VP Manufacturing Alix Nicholaeff
Senior Production Manager Joshua Smith
Senior Production Manager, Subsidiary Rights Lina s Palma-Temena

Weldon Owen would also like to thank Jessica Easto for copyediting and Karen Levy
for proofreading.

ISBN: 979-8-88674-009-7

Manufactured in China by Insight Editions
10 9 8 7 6 5 4 3 2 1

ROOTS of PEACE   ⊕ Replanted Paper

Insight Editions, in association with Roots of Peace, will plant two trees for each tree used in
the manufacturing of this book. Roots of Peace is an internationally renowned humanitarian
organization dedicated to eradicating land mines worldwide and converting war-torn lands into
productive farms and wildlife habitats. Roots of Peace will plant two million fruit and nut trees in
Afghanistan and provide farmers there with the skills and support necessary for sustainable land use.